THOMAS HARDY'S DORSET

THROUGH TIME

Steve Wallis

AMBERLEY PUBLISHING

Acknowledgements

I would like to express my thanks to the National Trust for assistance with my photography at Hardy's Cottage and Max Gate, and also to Andy Helmore and Graham Reeves for their help.

First published 2012

Amberley Publishing
The Hill, Stroud, Gloucestershire, GL5 4EP
www.amberley-books.com

ISBN 978 1 4456 0754 2 (print)

British Library Cataloguing in Publication Data.
A catalogue record for this book is available from the British Library.

Typesetting by Amberley Publishing.
Printed in Great Britain.

Introduction

If, like me, you live in Dorchester and spend time pottering around the surrounding countryside and villages, then Thomas Hardy can seem to be everywhere. Places where he lived and worked are visitor attractions, there are buildings that still show his influence, and a great many places featured in his novels.

He set his stories in a fictional part of the country called 'Wessex', but this is heavily based on Dorset and other counties of South West England (Wessex being the real name of the Saxon kingdom that covered this area). His narratives are full of places that are similar in description, and usually in name, to real settlements. So, for instance, Hardy's Emminster equates with the real Beaminster, and King's Bere is based on Bere Regis. His town of Casterbridge may not be immediately recognisable as Dorchester from its name, but the appearance of real buildings such as the King's Arms quickly gives it away.

In particular, if you know a particular part of Dorset in which he sets a piece of action, you can often recognise real locations that Hardy was thinking about as he wrote. In my case, I first read *Under the Greenwood Tree* when I had not long been living in the county, and was pleasantly surprised to find how easy it was to follow the Mellstock quire on their Christmas round through the Bockhamptons and Stinsford.

I was intrigued, then, by the idea of using the format of the Through Time series to look at these places, with the added bonus that most of the old pictures would have been taken in Hardy's lifetime and so would show places as he saw them. I have limited the material to Dorset, or 'South Wessex' as Hardy would have it, and have included places associated with Hardy's life, others that appear in his novels in one form or another, and also some views that tell something about the times and locality in which Hardy lived.

In doing so, I hope to give an idea just how many such places there are in Dorset – but please bear in mind that what is in this book is just a sample. Please also bear in mind that the dates given for the old pictures are usually guesses.

And one final and probably fanciful thought: I cannot help looking at some of the old pictures and wondering whether one of the passersby was Hardy himself.

Hardy's Life

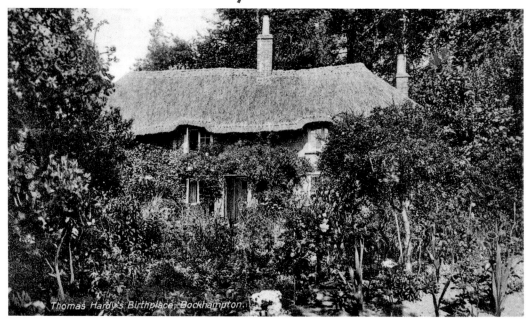

Higher Bockhampton, Hardy's Birthplace, c. 1920
Thomas Hardy was born in 1840 in the village of Higher Bockhampton, about 3 miles east of Dorchester as the crow flies. As this old postcard illustrates, the cottage in which he was born was already well known during his lifetime. It was built in 1799 by Hardy's great-grandfather, and was extended (to the right, as we look at it here) around the time of Thomas's birth.

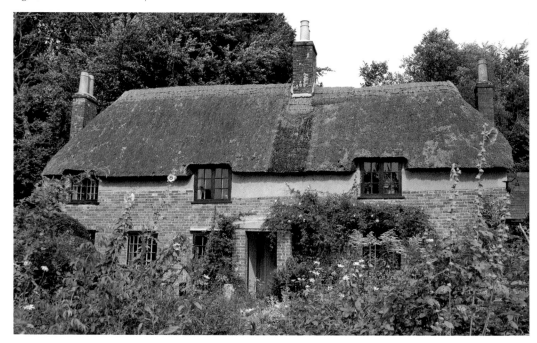

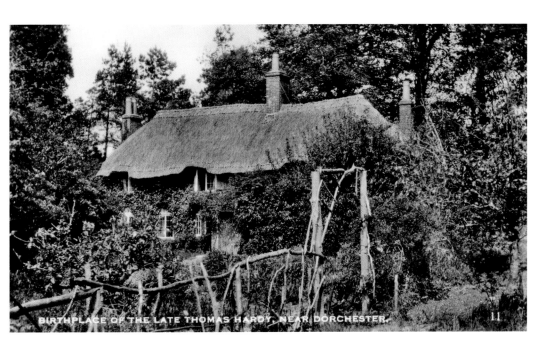

BIRTHPLACE OF THE LATE THOMAS HARDY, NEAR DORCHESTER.

Higher Bockhampton, Hardy's Birthplace, *c.* 1930

This second old photograph was probably taken within a few years of Hardy's death. The association with Hardy spared the cottage from major modernisation or even demolition, and today it is in the care of the National Trust. It sits at the end of the track that runs through the small but strung-out hamlet, and can be enjoyed as both Hardy's birthplace and an unspoilt 200-year-old cottage.

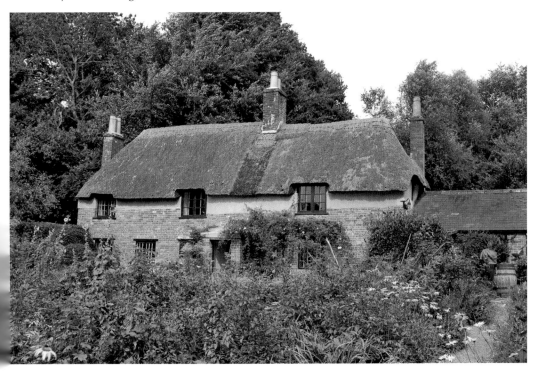

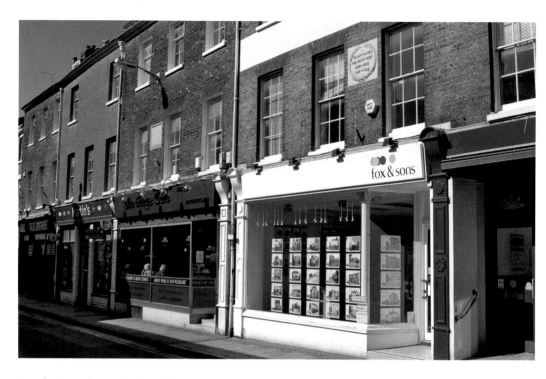

Dorchester, Plaques in South Street

Instead of going into the family building business, at the age of sixteen Thomas became a pupil of the Dorchester architect John Hicks. A plaque above the Gorge Café in South Street records the location of Hicks' office. While we are here, it is worth mentioning that the building next door has its own plaque at first-floor level, this one recording the residence there of William Barnes, about whom more later.

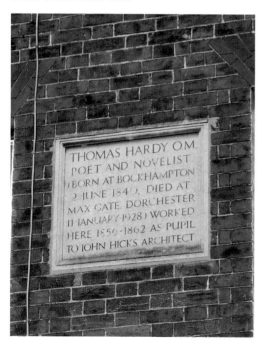

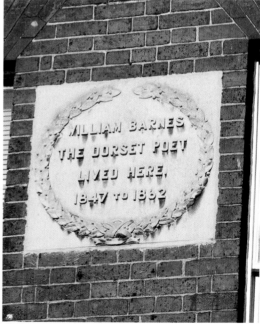

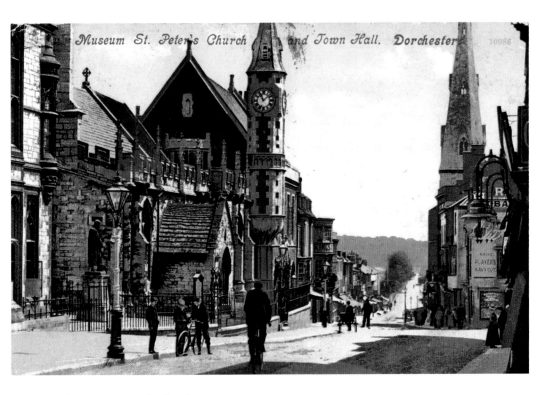

Dorchester, St Peter's Church, *c.* 1905

St Peter's church is in the middle of Dorchester and you can see much of it on the left of this view. It is the only one of the town's three medieval churches to survive largely intact. On display in the south chancel aisle is a copy of a plan of the church drawn by Hardy in 1856, the year in which he started with Hicks, who undertook a lot of church restoration.

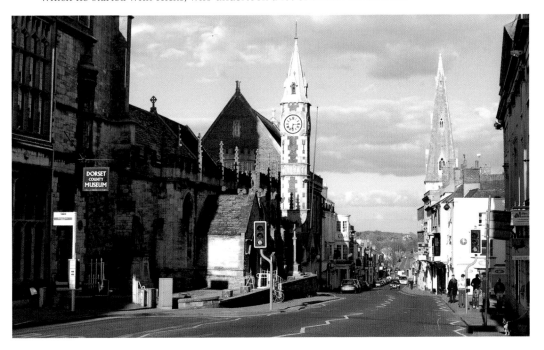

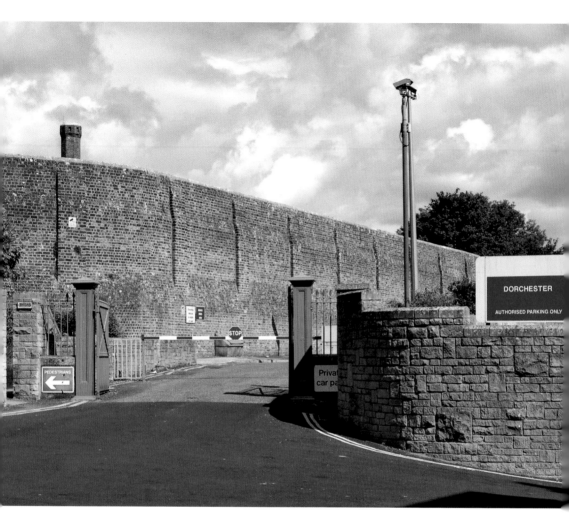

Dorchester, the Prison

What is seen as one of the formative moments of Hardy's youth took place in August 1856, only a couple of months after he joined Hicks. He witnessed the public hanging at Dorchester Prison of a woman called Martha Browne, who had killed her husband. Afterwards he was ashamed that he had been there, although as was common at the time he had been part of a large crowd. The sight has been blamed in part for Hardy's melancholy outlook on life, which comes across in his writings.

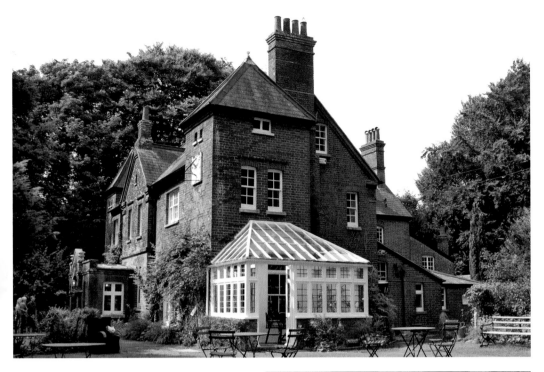

Dorchester, Max Gate

During his adult life Hardy had lived in a number of locations in Dorset and beyond. In 1885 he built himself a house on the south-eastern edge of Dorchester, where he lived for the rest of his life. It is beside the road to Wareham, which was originally a toll road. There had been a toll gate near this spot, manned by a chap by the surname of 'Mack', hence the house's name: Max Gate. Like his birthplace, the house is now in the care of the National Trust and open to visitors at particular times.

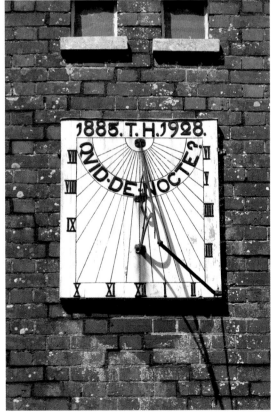

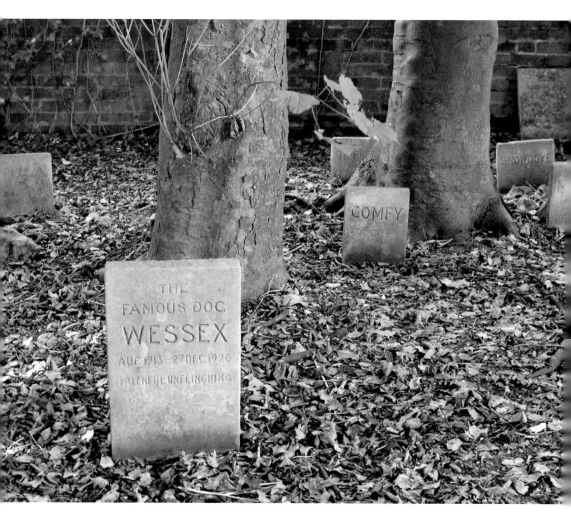

Dorchester, Pet Cemetery at Max Gate
On one side of the front garden at Max Gate, the visitor comes across this rather touching little sight. All the pets owned by Hardy that died while he and his two wives were living at the house are buried here. Each has its own tombstone, all but one of which were carved by Hardy himself.

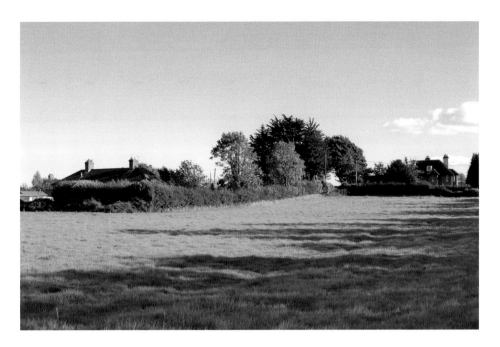

West Stafford, Talbothayes

Around 1890 Thomas designed a house for his brother Henry just east of West Stafford, which is itself a couple of miles east of Dorchester. Its name, 'Talbothayes', was used for nearby Lower Lewell Farm in *Tess of the D'Urbervilles*. Their sisters Mary and Kate also moved in soon after and spent the rest of their lives here. The house is on the right in the top picture. Although Talbothayes and Max Gate are the only surviving buildings known to have been designed by Hardy, it has been suggested that the nearby cottages, some of which are shown below, may also be his work.

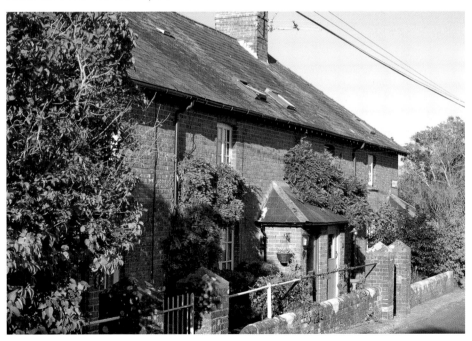

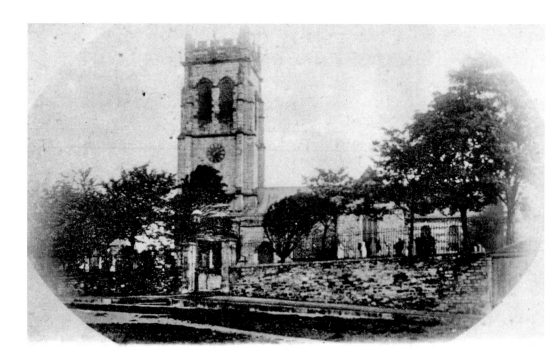

Fordington, St George's Church, c. 1905

Until the early nineteenth century, Fordington was a separate village from Dorchester, but during Hardy's lifetime it was being enveloped by the town's eastward expansion. Even today its parish church and the green in front look like part of a village. Hardy must have passed by regularly on his way into town from Max Gate. The old photograph shows a rather shorter church – the nave was extended and a new chancel added in works that lasted from 1907 until after the First World War.

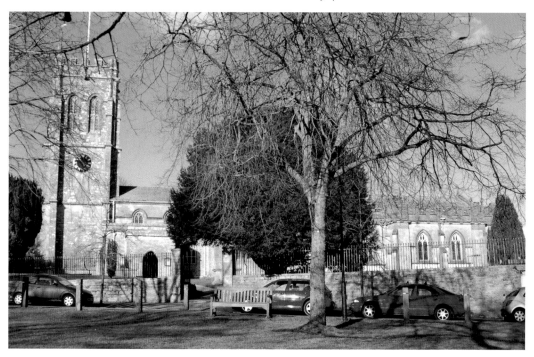

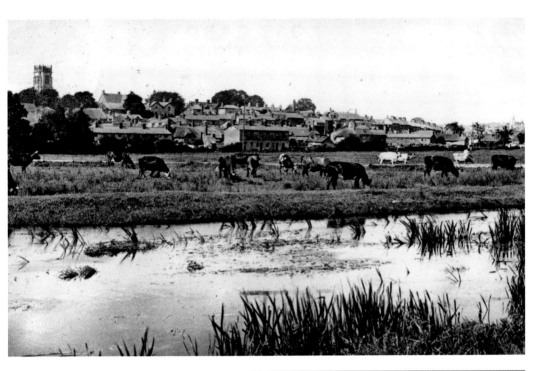

Fordington from the Watermeadows, c. 1900

Hardy had been on the church's restoration committee at an earlier stage. In 1901 the pinnacles on the church tower were replaced whilst Hardy was on holiday. He disliked one particular large octagonal pinnacle, which was of an incorrect architectural style, and resigned in protest. The pinnacle is on the nearest corner of the tower in my picture. The tower is at left in the old picture, which I think pre-dates the addition of the pinnacle (again, it would be at the nearest corner).

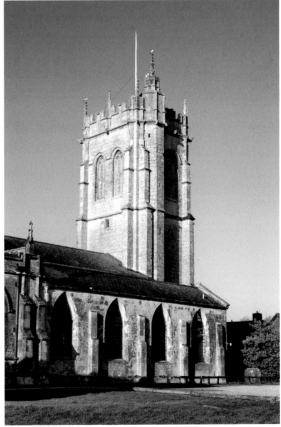

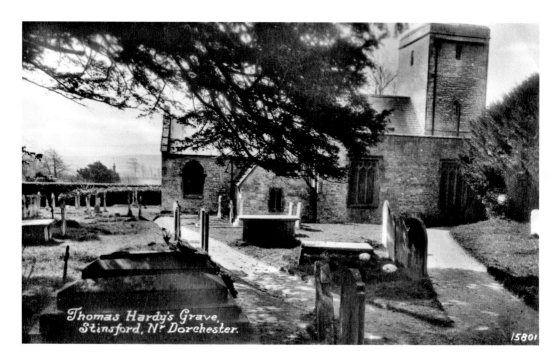

Stinsford, Churchyard, c. 1935

Hardy had wanted to be buried in Stinsford churchyard, as was the normal practice in his family. In the confusion after his death at Max Gate in January 1928, though, it was decided that such a national figure should be cremated and his remains interred in Poets' Corner at Westminster Abbey. The vicar of Stinsford came up with the idea that his heart at least should be buried at his church.

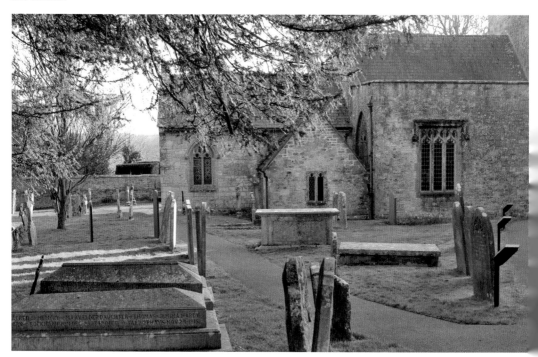

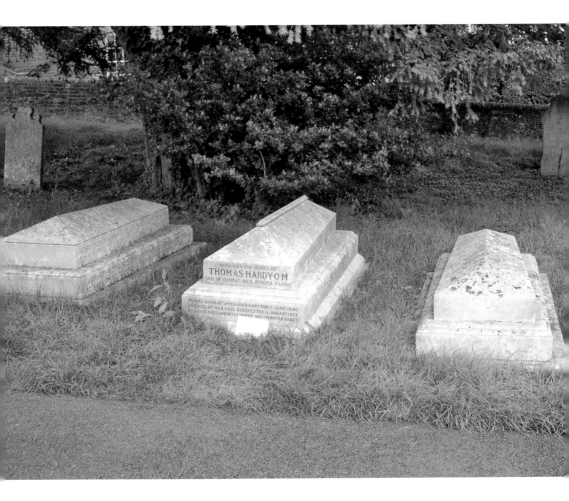

Stinsford, Hardy Family Graves

Here is a closer view of the graves that are in the left foreground of the previous pictures. The central one contains Hardy's heart, together with the remains of his wives, Emma and Florence. The one on the left contains the remains of his siblings, Henry, Mary and Kate, and that on the right is of his parents. Other Hardys are buried nearby.

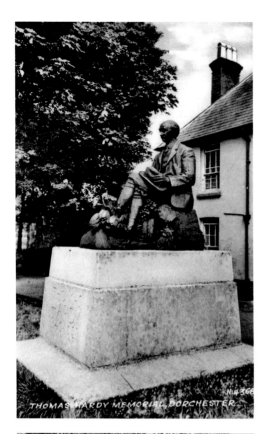

Dorchester, Statue of Hardy, c. 1935
In 1931, only three years after Hardy's death, the town with which he had so many associations erected this statue of him near Top O'Town. It is the work of the sculptor Eric Kennington, who was also a noted war artist.

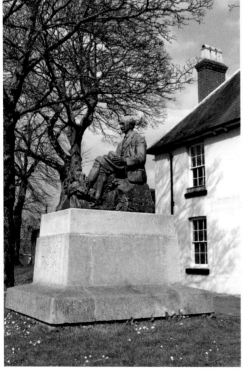

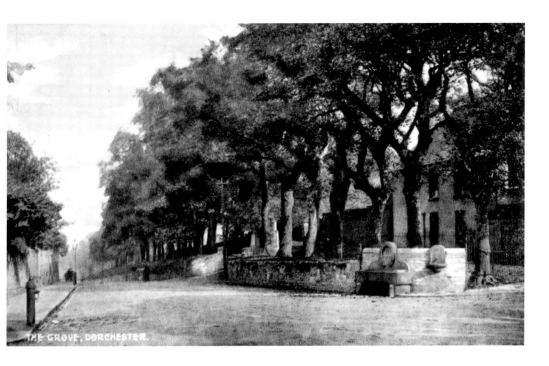

Dorchester, The Grove, c. 1905

Here is a pair of wider views of the location of the statue. The old picture looks down The Grove from the middle of what is now the Top O'Town roundabout, while mine was taken from the safety of the pavement. Differences between the two include the loss of the drinking trough and appearance of Hardy's statue on the right. Further to the left, the realignment of the entrance to Colliton Park presumably took place in connection with the building of County Hall.

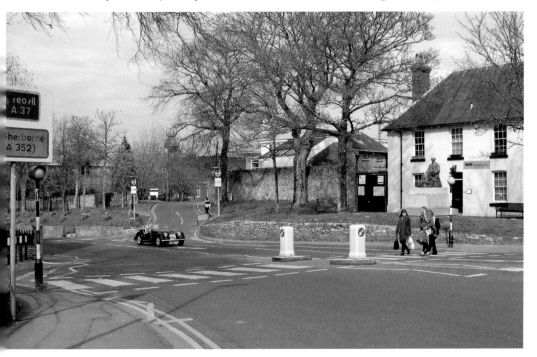

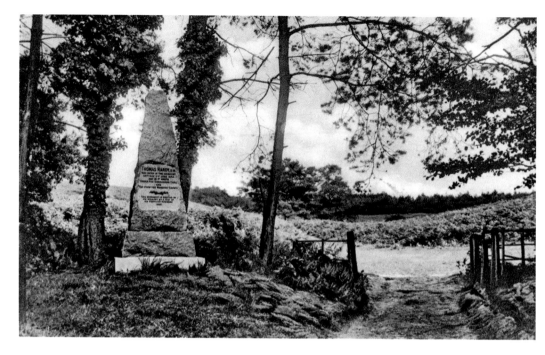

Higher Bockhampton, American Memorial, *c.* 1935

In the same year that the statue was erected, this memorial was set up outside Hardy's birthplace. As the inscription records, it was 'erected to his memory by a few of his American admirers'. The memorial was unveiled by a professor of both Oxford and Harvard Universities, and is testament to Hardy's worldwide popularity that continues today.

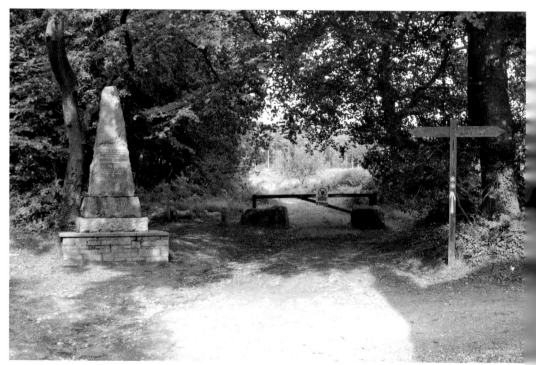

Hardy and History

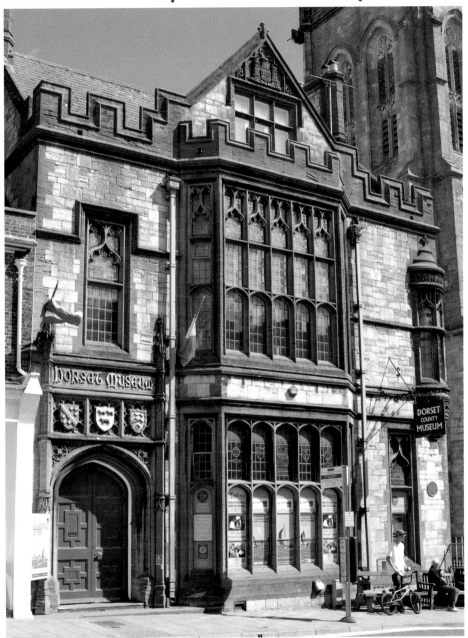

Dorchester, Dorset County Museum

Hardy's antiquarian interests link him strongly with the County Museum, which is in Dorchester's High West Street next to St Peter's church. It was constructed in the 1880s and Hardy was a frequent visitor, spending much time in the reading room. After his death his study at Max Gate was reconstructed in the museum and can still be seen there. The museum has recently obtained some of Hardy's manuscripts.

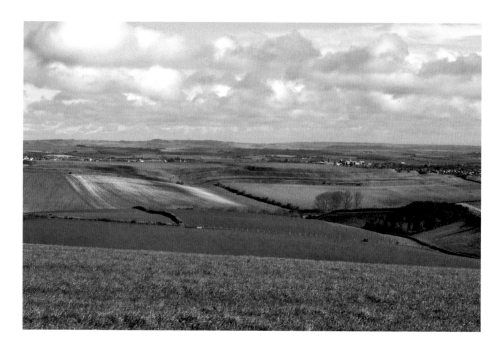

Maiden Castle

The Iron Age hillfort of Maiden Castle looms over the south-west side of Dorchester. It has been described as the best of its type in the country, and it is a spectacular place to visit. Hardy was as impressed as anyone, and he uses the name '*Mai Dun*', which meant 'Great Hill' in Celtic, and which could be the origin of the real name. In the 1880s a Roman temple was discovered and excavated within the hillfort, and in the decade after Hardy's death the famous archaeologist Sir Mortimer Wheeler undertook a major excavation campaign here. As a result of Wheeler's and later work at Maiden Castle, we now know a great deal more about the development of the site, which began over 2,000 years before the hillfort was constructed.

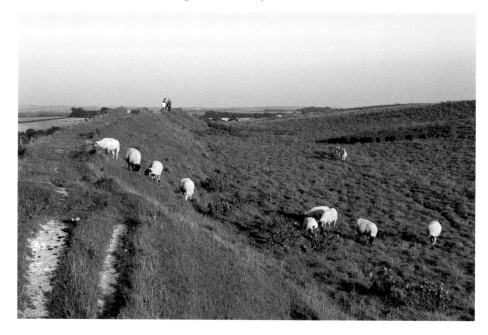

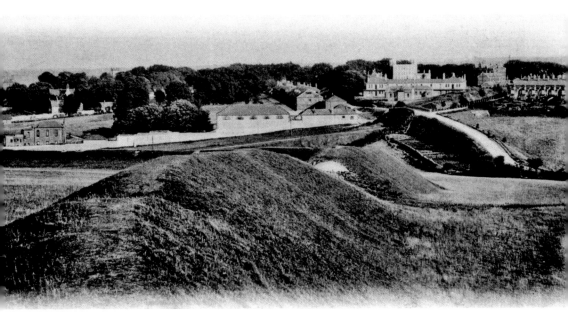

Dorchester, View Towards Town from Poundbury Camp, *c.* **1910**
Poundbury Camp is Dorchester's other Iron Age hillfort. It appears in Hardy's writings, especially his poetry, as 'Pummery' or 'Pummery-Tout'. 'Tout' is a common local name for a high lookout, which is appropriate for Poundbury, which overlooks the Frome valley. The view here also gives us a good look at the western part of the town, including in the old picture the once-extensive army barracks, about which more later.

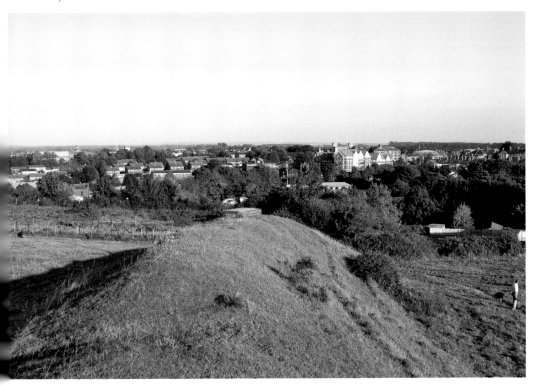

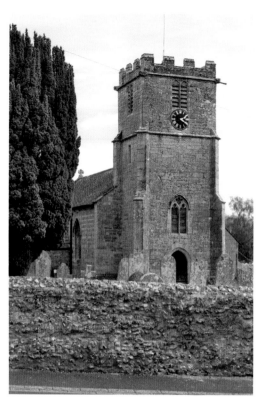

Conserving Parish Churches

In the early years of his architectural career, Hardy had seen some very heavy-handed 'restoration' taking place on medieval churches. He tried to put things right in later life. When in 1889 he heard of a proposal to demolish the church at Stratton (above), 3 miles north-west of Dorchester, he was heavily involved in a successful campaign that prevented this and led to a sympathetic restoration. His reputation led to him being asked to supervise the 1894 restoration of the church at West Knighton (below), 3 miles south-east of the county town.

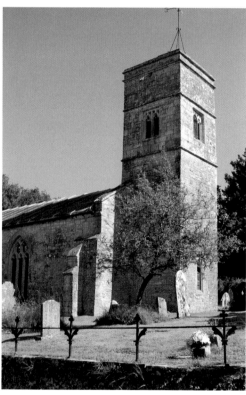

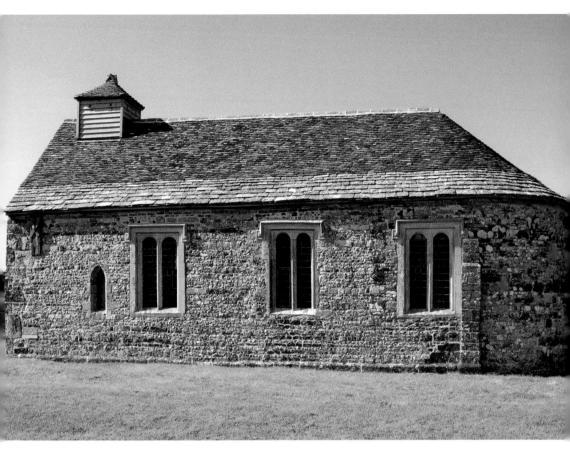

Winterborne Tomson, Parish Church

Even after his death Hardy was able to help in the preservation of this beautiful little Norman church. Winterborne Tomson is the furthest downstream but one of the north Winterborne villages, and lies just off the road between Bere Regis and Wimborne Minster. It is really no more than a hamlet, so there was probably little money available for its upkeep. In 1929 the local architect A. R. Powys found it being used as an animal pen, and decided to restore it. Much of the funding came from the sale of one of Hardy's manuscripts, and the work was completed in 1931. Today it is in the care of the Churches Conservation Trust and is well worth hunting out, not just for the exterior but also the Georgian woodwork of box pews and the like inside.

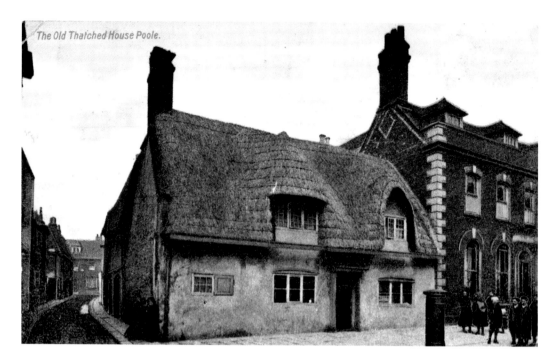

The Old Thatched House Poole.

Poole, the Old Thatched House, c. 1910

Now for two pairs of views taken in Poole, which illustrate the contrasting fortunes of historic buildings in the town that Hardy called 'Havenpool'. We tend to think that historic buildings in our towns and cities were lost during the twentieth century as the result of Second World War bombing and 1960s town planning, but this fine example that stood on the corner of High Street and Carter Lane was actually demolished in 1919.

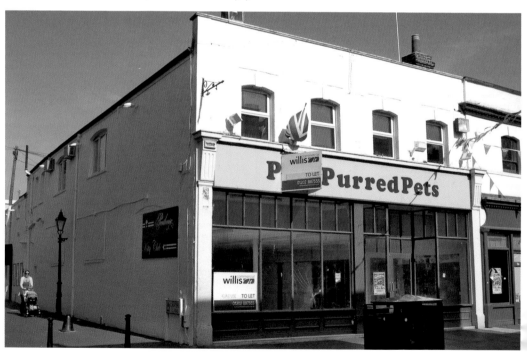

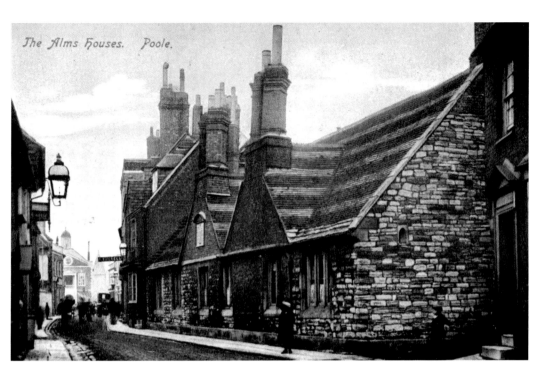

The Alms Houses. Poole.

Poole, St George's Almshouses, *c.* 1905
Hardy would have been happier with this example. These buildings in Church Street were built in the early fifteenth century to house priests of the nearby St James's parish church. They became almshouses after the Reformation and, as a plaque on the frontage records, were restored in 1904. The Guildhall is in the background of these views.

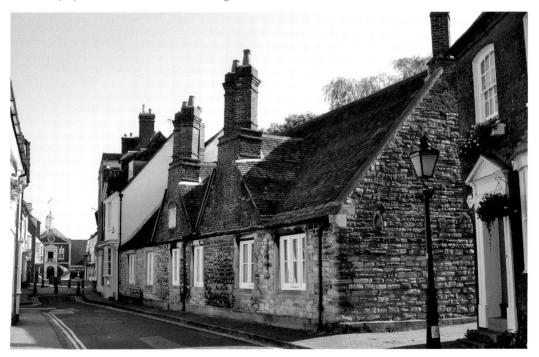

Hardy's Times

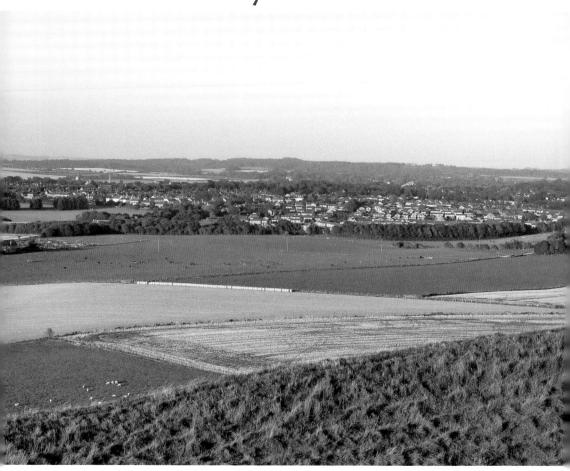

Dorchester Seen from Maiden Castle

As the first chapter illustrates, Dorchester was the setting for much of Hardy's own life. Under the name of 'Casterbridge', it was also one of the main settings for his novels. Here we look from Maiden Castle, at one time almost a town in its own right, across Dorchester. For much of its history Dorchester was confined within the walls of its Roman predecessor, Durnovaria, but during Hardy's lifetime it underwent considerable expansion. Much of this was due to the Duchy of Cornwall, the owner of much of the land immediately outside the town, which began releasing land for development, especially to the south and west, around the 1870s.

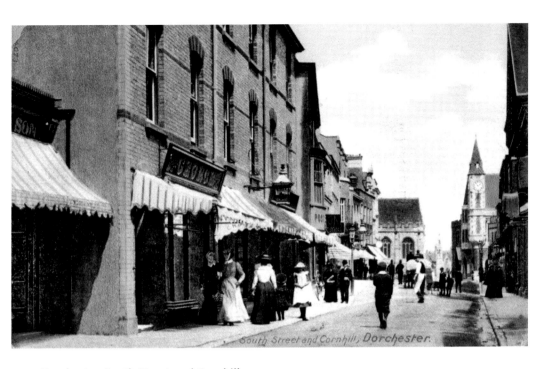

Dorchester, South Street and Cornhill, *c.* 1905

Here is a scene within the busy market town. We are looking up South Street and through Cornhill with parts of St Peter's church and the Corn Exchange in the distance. A livestock market was held in Cornhill until the 1850s, when it was moved out to Fair Field, south of the town centre. My picture may give the impression that Dorchester is now less bustling than in Hardy's day, but it was taken on a Sunday morning!

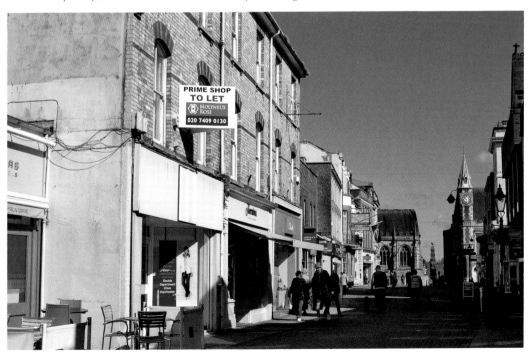

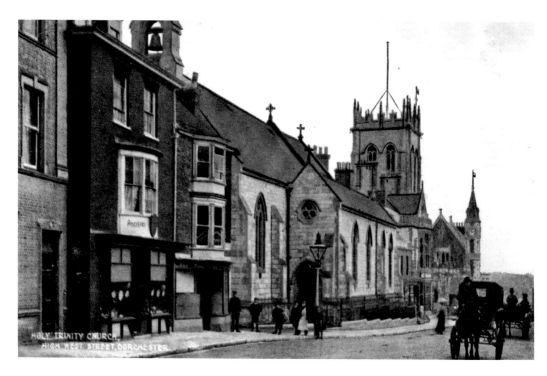

Dorchester, Holy Trinity Church, c. 1905

Now we go to the top of Cornhill and turn left into High West Street. Some way along, we look back for this view, of which the centrepiece is Holy Trinity church. Together with St Peter's and All Saints churches, it was one of Dorchester's three medieval parish churches. The structure was rebuilt in the 1820s, and then again in 1875–76. The second rebuild was by the architect Benjamin Ferrey, who undertook much work in Dorset and beyond.

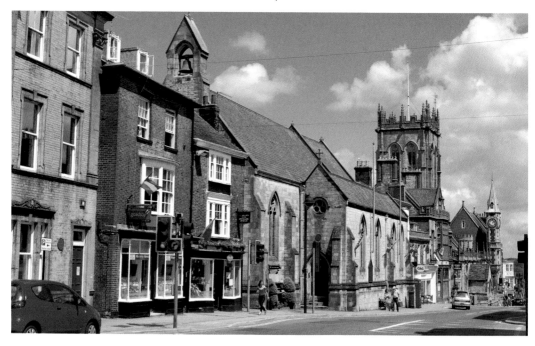

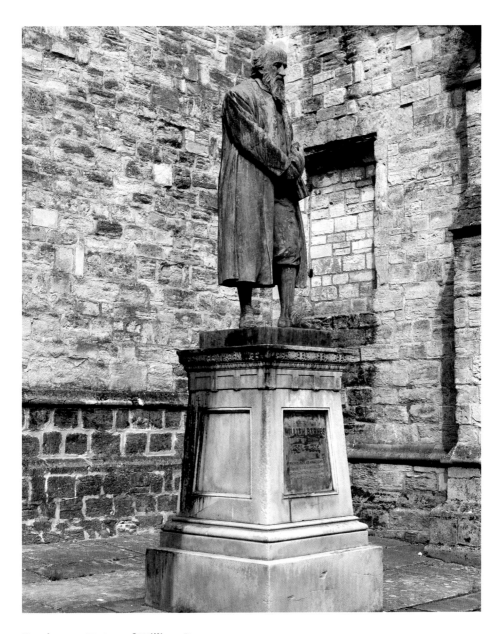

Dorchester, Statue of William Barnes

This statue stands in front of St Peter's church, and commemorates an older friend of Hardy's and a man of note in his own right. William Barnes was born in 1801 in the north of the county near Sturminster Newton. He was running a school in Dorchester when Hardy began his architectural training, and he later became rector of the nearby village of Winterborne Came, where he is buried. Like Hardy he wrote poetry, in his case in the dialect of north Dorset, which differed somewhat from the generally south Dorset speech of Hardy's characters. Barnes also shared Hardy's antiquarian interests, and was one of the leading figures of a campaign during Isambard Kingdom Brunel's construction of the railway line down to Weymouth in the 1850s. This campaign prevented the demolition of the Maumbury Rings monument in Dorchester, and persuaded Brunel to tunnel under Poundbury hillfort rather than dig a cutting through it. The statue was erected in 1888, two years after Barnes' death.

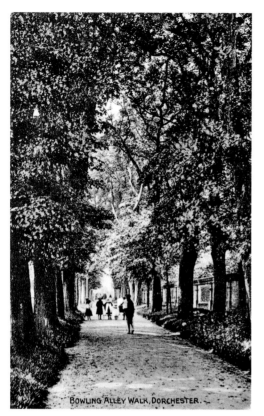

BOWLING ALLEY WALK, DORCHESTER.

Bowling Alley Walk, *c.* 1920
The Walks are a unique feature of
Dorchester. The Roman town defences were
maintained at least until the Civil War in
the mid-seventeenth century, but soon after
changes in warfare made them obsolete. The
town, which in Hardy's novels can seem like
a rural backwater, actually followed the latest
Continental fashions in the early eighteenth
century, laying out the Walks along those
defences. Bowling Alley Walk, seen here, is
at the western end of the south side of the
Roman town.

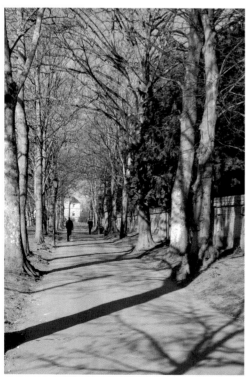

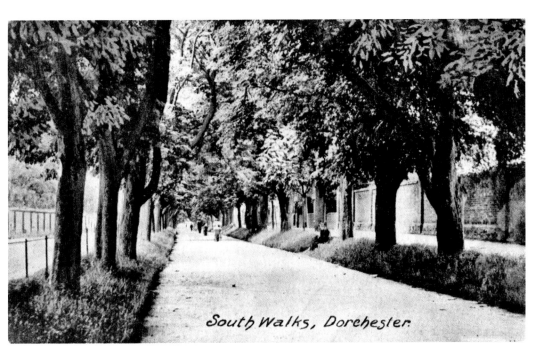

South Walks, Dorchester.

Dorchester, South Walks, *c.* 1905

Here we are further east along the south side, and this view gives an idea of how the Roman defences were adapted. The top of the massive inner bank was levelled off and the tree-lined path laid out on top. The ditch immediately outside the bank was filled in, and the road that we see on the left was constructed on top of it.

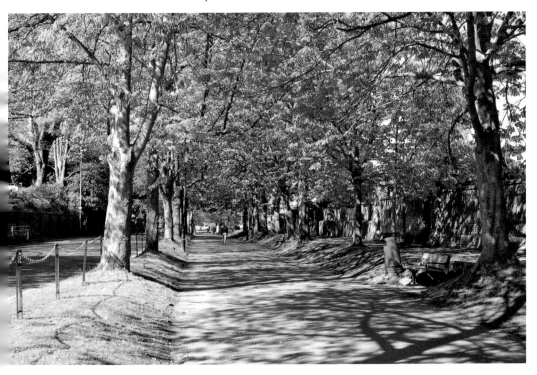

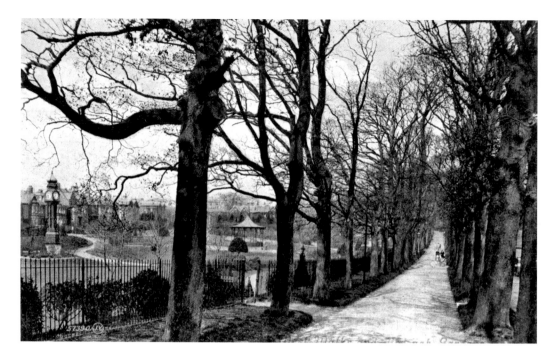

Borough Gardens from West Walks, *c.* 1910

As towns and cities expanded during the late nineteenth century, access to healthy countryside became more difficult for the inhabitants. So it became fashionable for parks to be laid out as places to enjoy and get a bit of exercise. Dorchester was no exception, and the Borough Gardens on the west side of the town were opened in July 1896. They were designed by the landscape architect and naturalist William Golding of the Royal Botanic Gardens at Kew, who undertook several hundred such projects during his career.

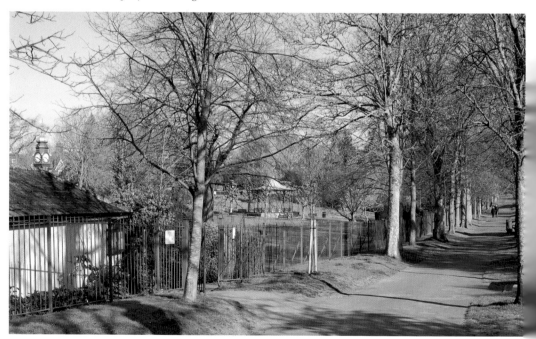

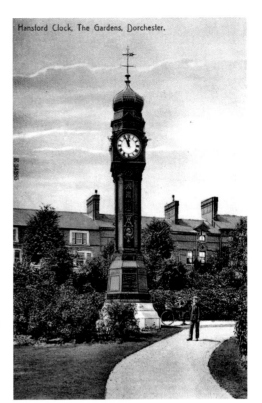

Dorchester, Clock in the Borough Gardens, c. 1910

Several features were added to the gardens in their early years. A local man, Charles Hansford, paid for both a fountain and the clock we see here, which were erected in 1905. Such donations were seen as a public service, although there must have been an element of showing off in many cases. The green of the structure in the old picture seems odd – perhaps someone artificially coloured the image without knowing what the real colours were.

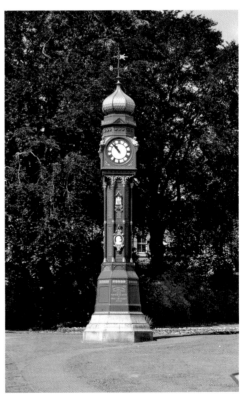

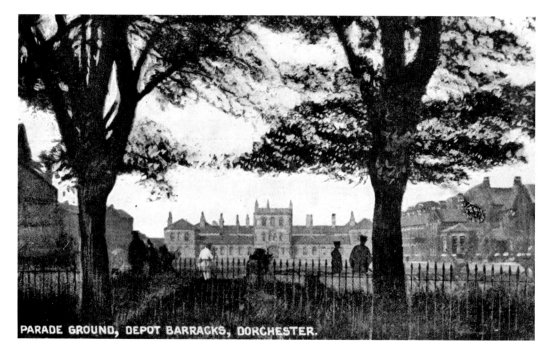

PARADE GROUND, DEPOT BARRACKS, DORCHESTER.

Dorchester, the Barracks, c. 1925

There had been an Army garrison at Dorchester since the eighteenth century, and in the 1870s a new barracks was built for the newly formed Dorsetshire Regiment on the north side of Bridport Road. The old picture looks from Bridport Road across the parade ground towards the north-west block. This view is now obscured by the tax office, and mine was taken from closer to that block.

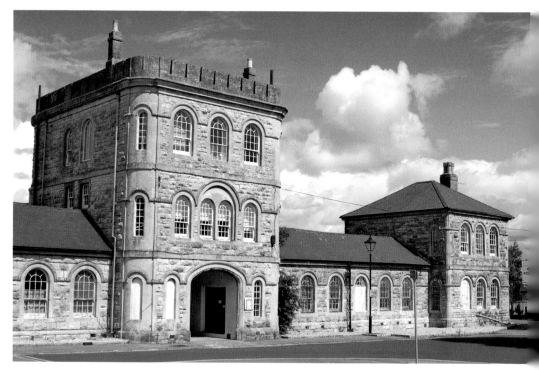

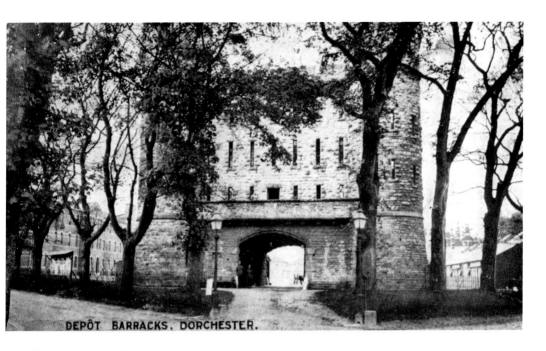

DEPÔT BARRACKS, DORCHESTER.

Dorchester, the Keep, c. 1900

The Keep as it is now known was constructed in 1876–77 as the very showy gatehouse to the barracks. It now houses the Military Museum of Devon & Dorset. Note the trees lining Bridport Road in the foreground of this old photograph and the previous one. Local legend has it that these and other trees lining the roads leading out of Dorchester were planted by French prisoners during the Napoleonic Wars, although some are actually of later date. Most of those in Bridport Road were cut down not long after these photographs were taken.

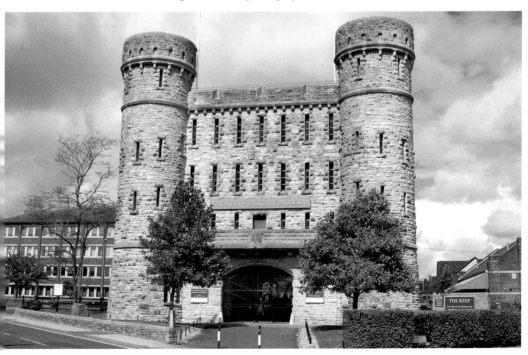

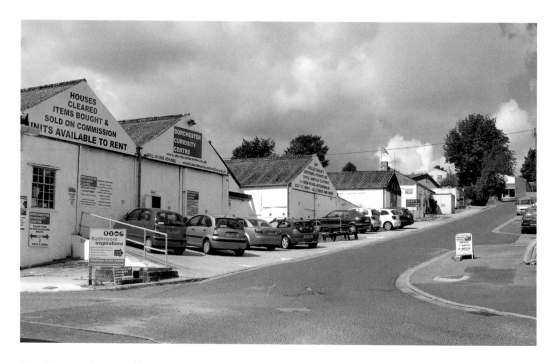

Dorchester, First World War German Prisoners

During the First World War there was a prisoner-of-war camp in Dorchester down the hill from the Army barracks. The barracks of the German prisoners were built on terraces cut into the slope below Poundbury Camp. The Grove Trading Estate (*above*) is built on this terracing. Hardy befriended some of the prisoners and paid them to work in his garden. A memorial to those prisoners, who died during their captivity, can still be seen in Fordington cemetery (*below*).

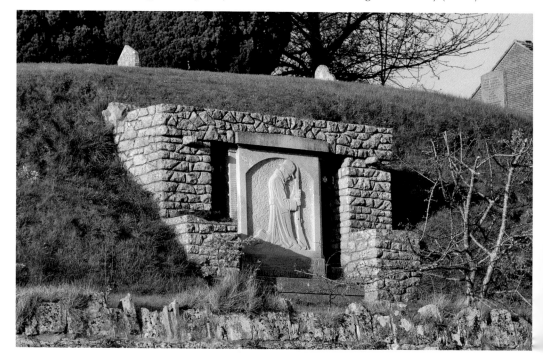

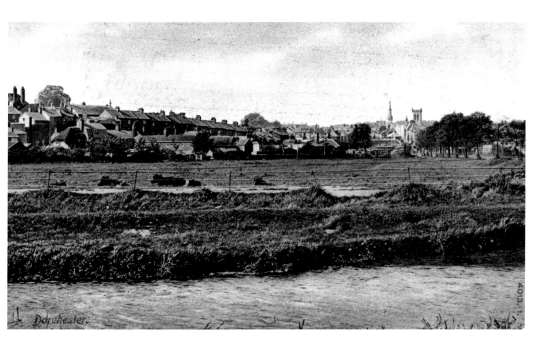

Dorchester from the Watermeadows, *c.* 1905

One of the familiar sights of Hardy's lifetime that has almost been lost today is the 'drowning' of the watermeadows along the Frome valley. In late winter and early spring, water from the river was diverted through a complex series of channels to flow like a sheet across the ground, before being taken back to the river through more channels. This deposited nutrients and prevented frosts forming, so that grass grew earlier in the year. In this old photograph, some of these channels can be made out in the field beyond the river.

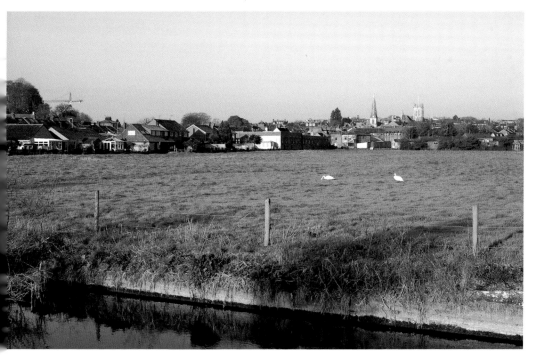

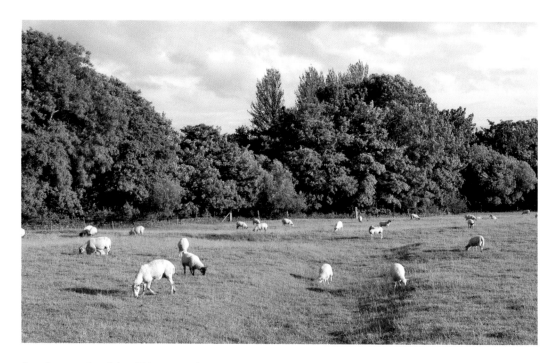

Dorchester, Surviving Watermeadow Features

The heyday of the watermeadows was the later eighteenth and the nineteenth centuries. Towards the end of the Hardy's lifetime they were becoming obsolete due to the introduction of chemical fertilisers and other changes in agricultural practice, and around Dorchester they went out of use soon after the Second World War. However, we can still see the channels as earthworks all over the valley bottom, and sometimes even the sluices and hatches that were used to control the flow of the water.

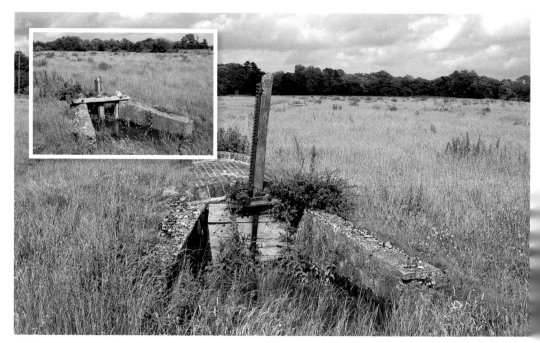

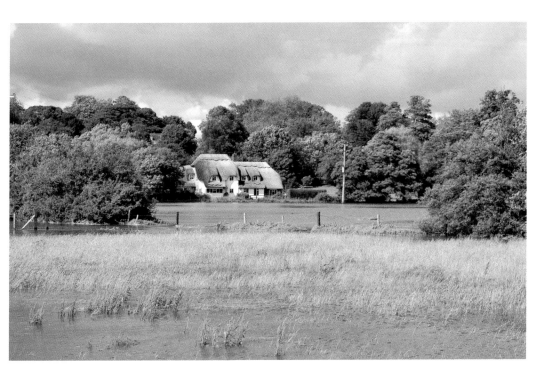

Dorchester, Watermeadows Between Dorchester and Stinsford

Today the occasional flood in the Frome valley can give us some idea of what the watermeadows would have looked like when drowned. Of course, drowning was a much more controlled process than we see in these photographs taken during the floods of July 2012.

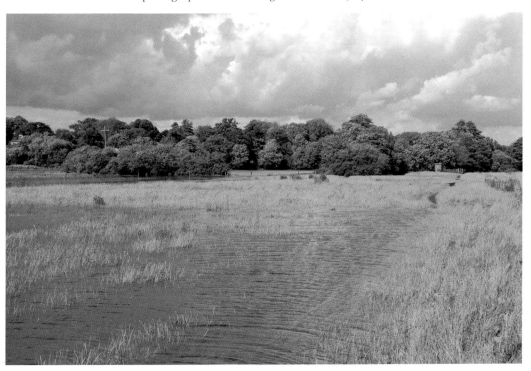

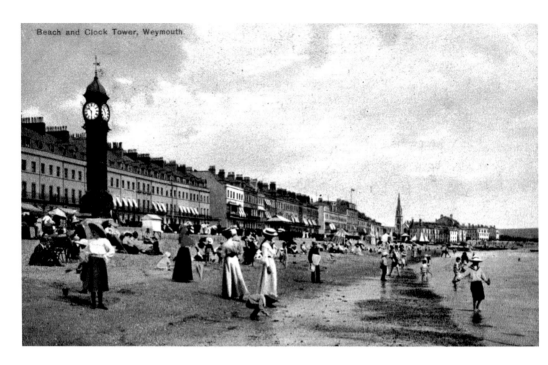

Beach and Clock Tower, Weymouth.

Weymouth, Seafront, *c.* 1910

Unsurprisingly considering its proximity to Dorchester, Hardy had a number of links with Weymouth. For instance, he lodged here for several months in 1869–70 while working for the Weymouth architect George Crickmay, and the town features in several novels as Budmouth or Budmouth Regis. The buildings of the Esplanade that we see here are mostly Georgian, but some date from Hardy's time, including the Jubilee Clock on the left, erected to celebrate Queen Victoria's Golden Jubilee of 1887, and St John's church in the distance, built in the 1850s.

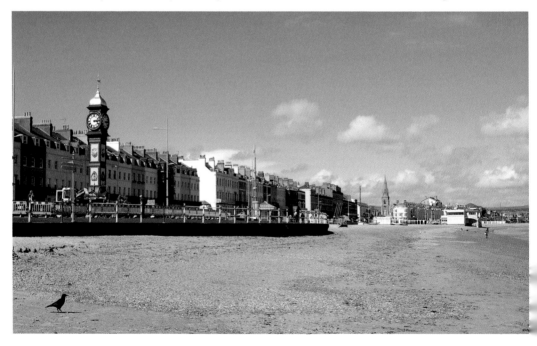

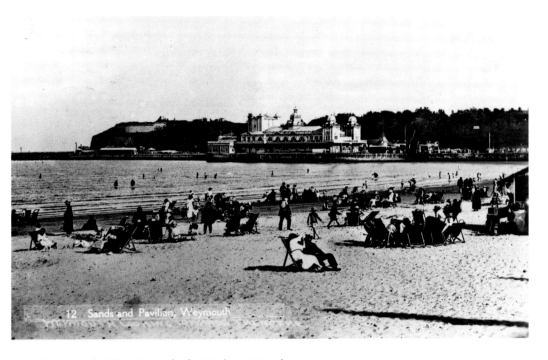

12 Sands and Pavilion, Weymouth

Weymouth, View Towards the Harbour Mouth, *c.* 1920

From the last viewpoint we turn around and head south a little way for this view. The building in the centre of the old picture is the original Weymouth Pavilion. This theatre was opened in 1908 and unfortunately destroyed by fire in 1954. Its replacement was built in 1960. To its left, and across the harbour mouth, we see Nothe Fort.

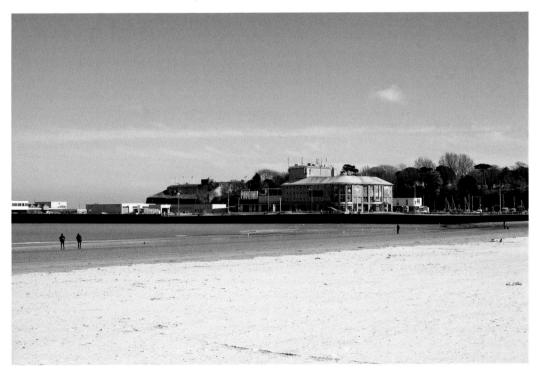

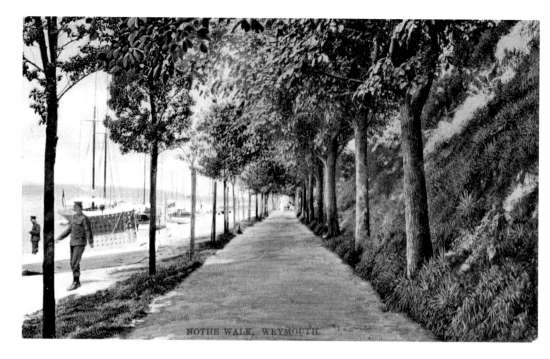

NOTHE WALK, WEYMOUTH.

Weymouth, Nothe Walk, *c.* 1905

In this view we look seaward along Nothe Walk, the path on the north side of Nothe Fort, with the harbour on our left. The fort was constructed in 1872 to protect that harbour and Portland Harbour on its other side as part of former Prime Minister Palmerston's plans for coastal defence. It was an important British and American base in the Second World War and is now a museum. 'Nothe' is a common name in Dorset for a headland – Hardy was of the view that it was simply a corruption of 'nose'.

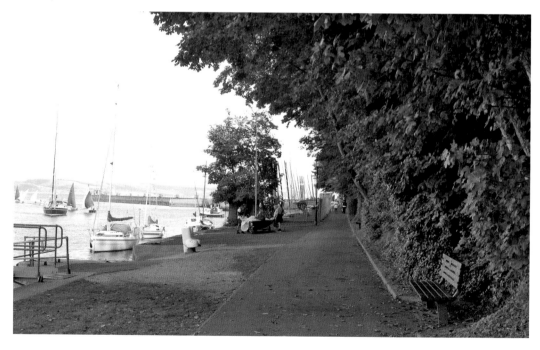

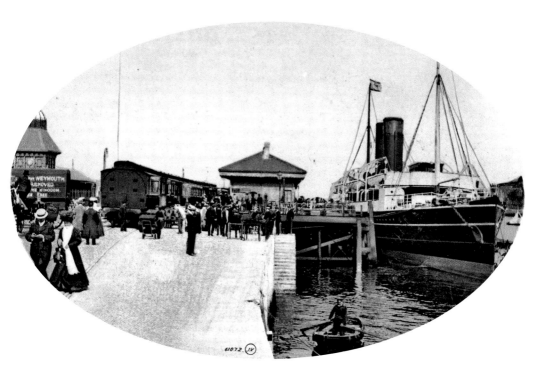

Weymouth, Ferry Terminal, c. 1905

Back across the harbour, we find the ferry terminal. Ferries had been sailing between Weymouth and the Channel Islands since 1794, and in 1889 a railway link was opened. As we see here, this brought trains right to the terminal along a line that branched off near the town's main station and looped around the inner side of the harbour. This line went out of use in the 1980s.

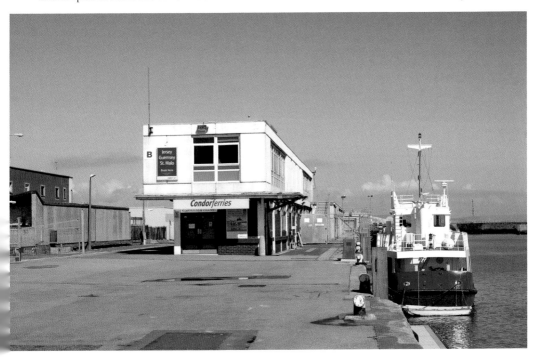

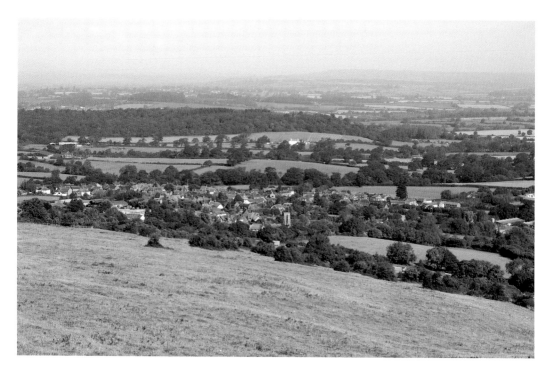

Blackmore Vale, Views from Okeford and Ibberton Hills

This broad vale occupies much of northern Dorset, as well as smaller areas of Somerset and Wiltshire. The greater part of it is drained by the River Stour. 'The Vale of the Little Dairies' is the usual Hardy term for it, although he does call it the 'Vale of Blakemore or Blackmoor' in *Tess of the D'Urbervilles*. Here we look across the vale from two locations on the chalk escarpment that forms its southern boundary.

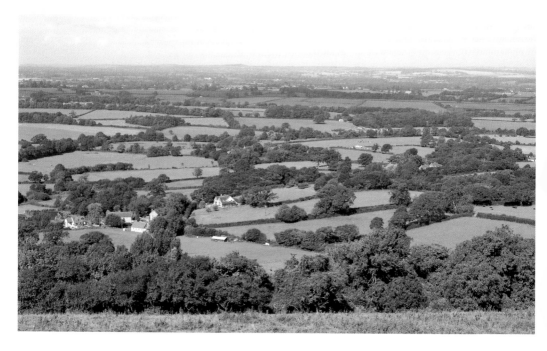

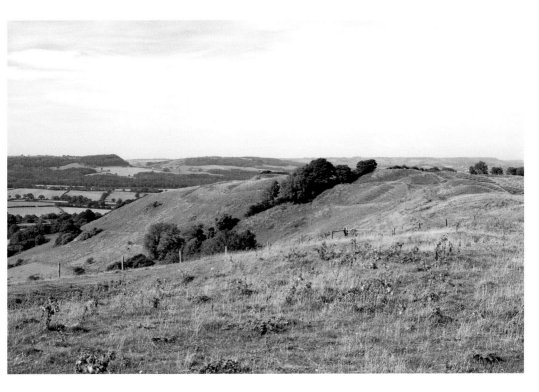

Blackmore Vale, Views from Near Rawlsbury Camp

The highest point on that escarpment, and nearly the highest in Dorset, is the famed Bulbarrow Hill. Close by the less well-known Iron Age hill fort of Rawlsbury Camp occupies a spur of land that projects into the Vale. Down in the clay vale, there has not been too much intensive arable farming, and the field pattern is one that Hardy would have recognised.

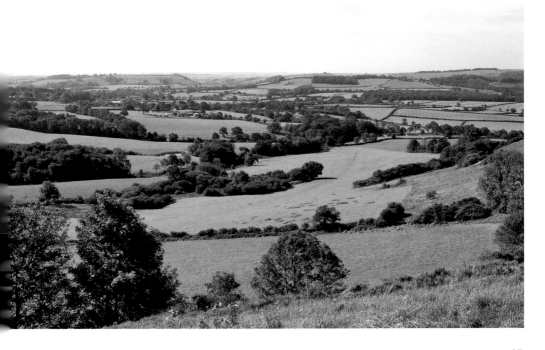

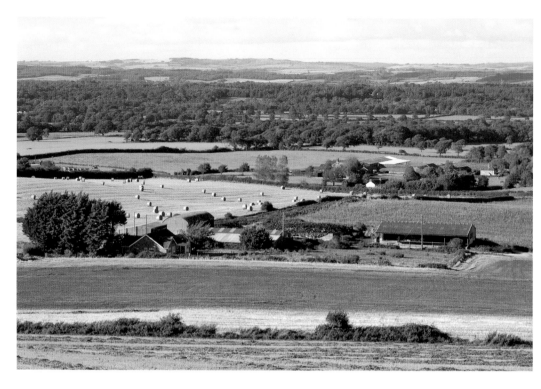

Vale of the Great Dairies

Here is Hardy's other Dorset vale. The 'Vale of the Great Dairies' is essentially that of the River Frome, which broadens out to the east of Dorchester on the way to Poole Harbour. The upper photograph looks north across this land from Lord's Barrow on the road to West Chaldon, and the lower looks from Bockhampton Bridge.

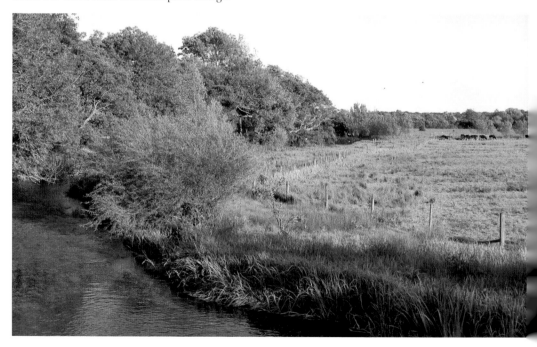

Locations Used in the Novels

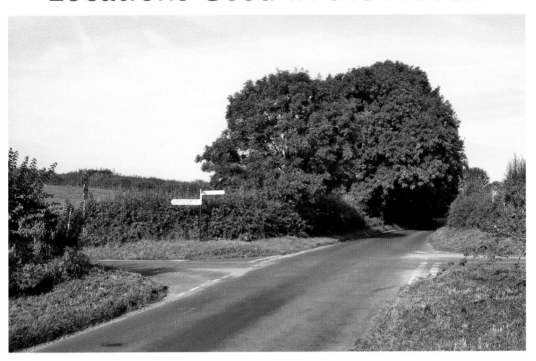

Between Higher and Lower Bockhampton, Crossroads

This chapter looks at some of those real places that can be picked out when reading Hardy novels. I will begin with the example I mentioned in the introduction – the opening chapters of *Under the Greenwood Tree*. Much of the novel is set in the parish of 'Mellstock', which is based on the parish of Stinsford, and the settlements of Stinsford itself and Higher and Lower Bockhampton just east of Dorchester. The story starts with the hero, Dick Dewey, heading home one Christmas Eve. He meets several characters at Mellstock Cross and together they head to Dewey's home at Upper Mellstock. The crossroads seen here between Higher and Lower Bockhampton must be the one Hardy had in mind. It is ironic that today the sign points to 'Hardy's Cottage', for it is his own birthplace that Hardy describes as the home of the Dewey family.

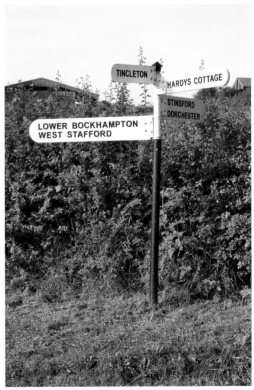

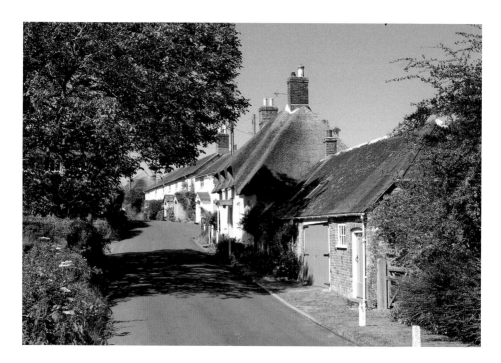

Lower Bockhampton

The group assembling at the Dewey residence is the village quire, the band that played during church services. They are about to follow the Christmas night tradition of going around the parish to play (and celebrate with) the local population. After visiting various outlying locations they come to the 'main village' of Lower Mellstock, which is our Lower Bockhampton. Here are two views of it, and on the left in the lower is the former village school, from which the new schoolteacher, Fancy Day, emerges in the story.

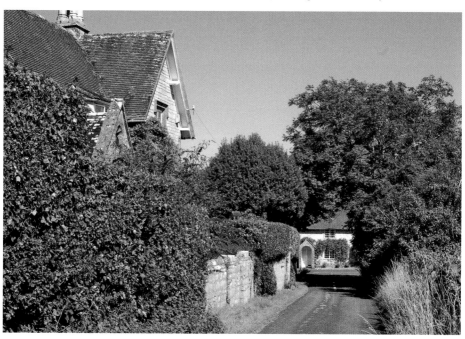

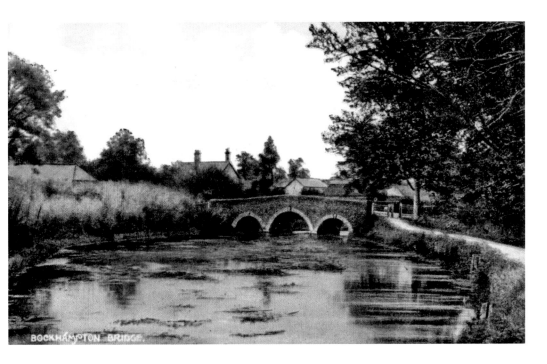

BOCKHAMPTON BRIDGE.

Lower Bockhampton, Bridge, *c.* 1900

The quire leaves the village by crossing 'Mellstock Bridge', and here at the southern end of the real Lower Bockhampton is Bockhampton Bridge, which dates from the late eighteenth century. It is said locally that Hardy's grandfather built the bridge, and since he reached adulthood in the latter years of that century and was a builder by trade, it seems entirely possible that he was at least involved in the construction.

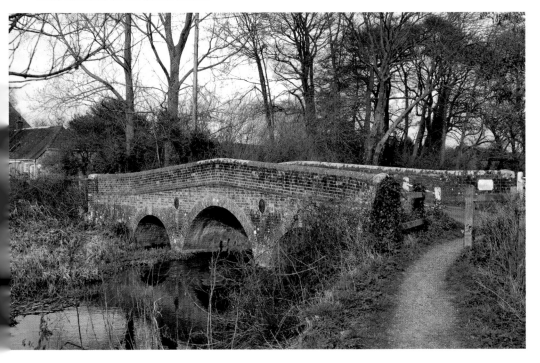

49

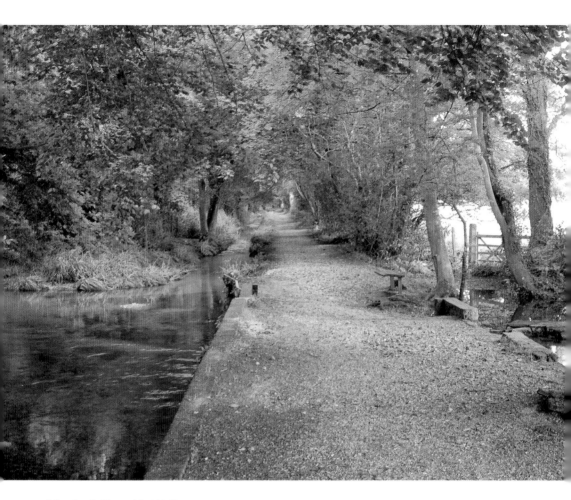

Stinsford, Riverside Walk
They then take an 'embowered path beside the Froom' on the way to the parish church and vicarage, and here is that path. It is still a favourite walk of many local people and eventually leads into Dorchester. Beside it is the main channel of the River Frome, the spelling of which Hardy has altered slightly, but the pronunciation is the same.

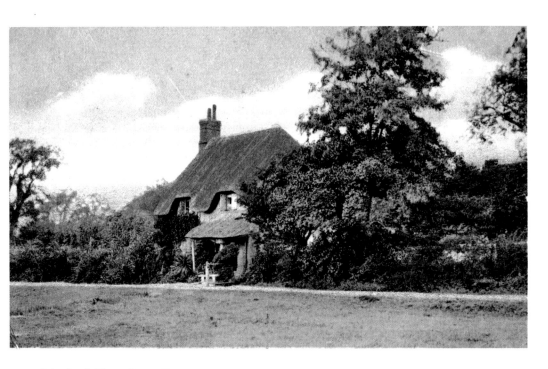

Stinsford, Three Bears Cottage, c. 1930
The party would have turned off the path to head up to the parish church just before the lovely building we see here, which is now called Three Bears Cottage. The real path used to be called Bockhampton Path, and leads directly to Grey's Bridge at the north-eastern corner of Dorchester.

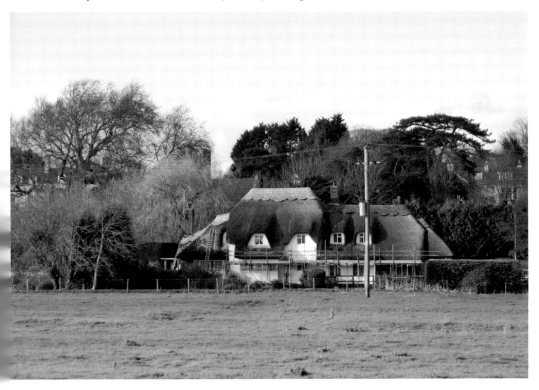

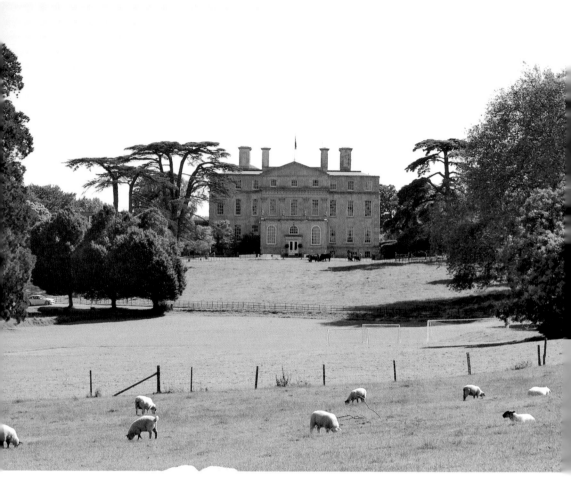

Kingston Maurward

Throughout all this, the characters are almost making a circuit outside the grounds of Kingston Maurward House, but it is not mentioned in the novel. There is, though, a passing reference to the 'Manor House', which may refer to the sixteenth-century Old Manor House that lies in the grounds. Kingston Maurward House itself was constructed in the early eighteenth century and re-faced in stone in the latter years of the same century. American troops were billeted here during the Second World War and today it is the main building of Kingston Maurward College.

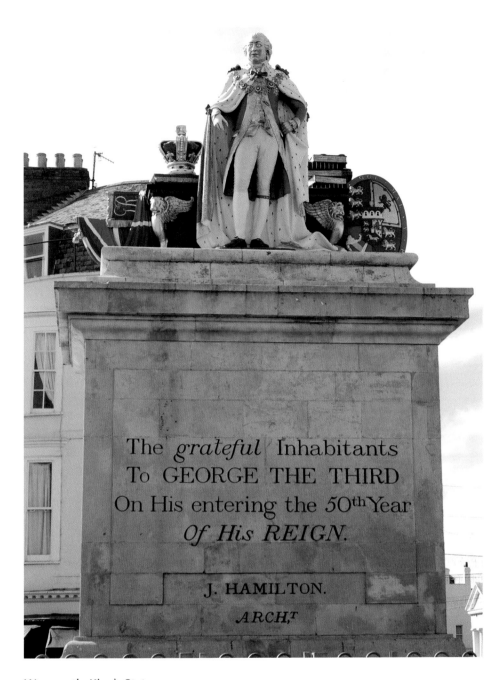

The **grateful** Inhabitants
To GEORGE THE THIRD
On His entering the 50th Year
Of His REIGN.

J. HAMILTON.

ARCH,ᵀ

Weymouth, King's Statue

Here is another passage from later on in *Under the Greenwood Tree* that we can follow. Dick sees Fancy Day in Budmouth and offers her a lift back to Mellstock. The location is the 'corner of Mary Street ... near the King's statue'. Here is the King's Statue in Weymouth, at a junction of roads that include St Mary Street. It was erected in 1809/10 to mark the fiftieth year of the reign of King George III, whose patronage had encouraged the development of the town as a holiday resort. The architect of the whole monument was the local man James Hamilton. The statue itself was the work of John Sealy – it was constructed of the artificial Coade stone invented by Sealy's cousin Eleanor Coade.

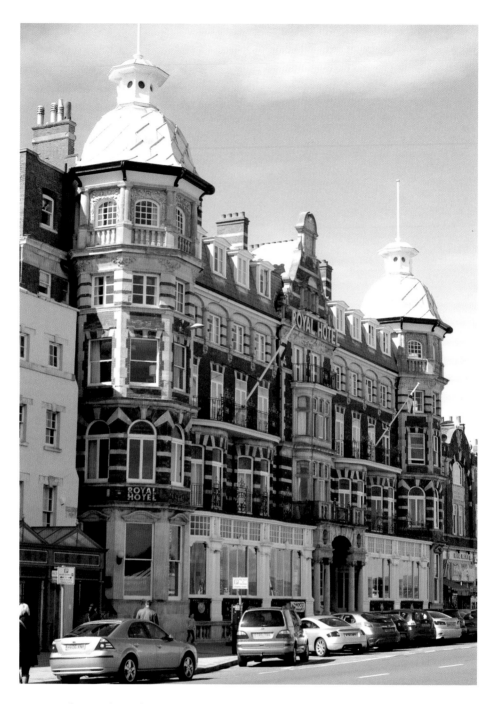

Weymouth, Royal Hotel

Fancy accepts the offer of a lift and they set off past the 'Old Royal Hotel' where King George III had attended events. A short distance from the King's Statue on the Esplanade is the Royal Hotel. The building we see today was constructed between 1897 and 1899, a quarter of a century after Hardy wrote the novel and over half a century after the time in which it was set. However, this building was built on the site of another Royal Hotel which the King did indeed visit.

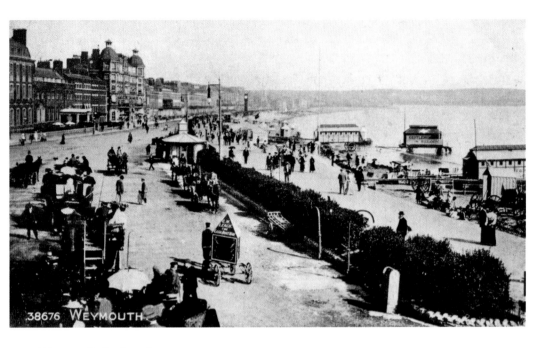

Weymouth, Esplanade, *c.* 1910

This pair of photographs shows the section of the Esplanade where this takes place. The old photograph was, I believe, taken from a second-floor window or the roof of the Statue House. Not only is it a charming view, with bathing machines and the like, but the Royal Hotel is the prominent building on the left, and the King's Statue is just out of view further to the left. My shot was taken from the little grass island in front of the statue.

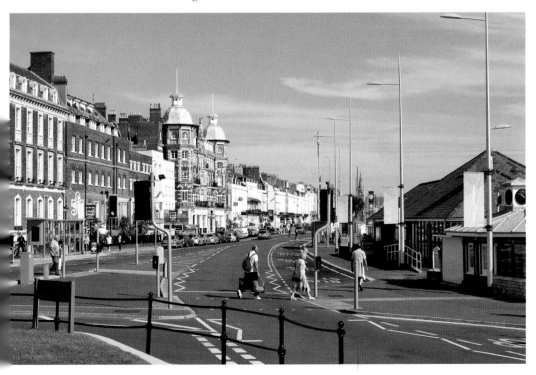

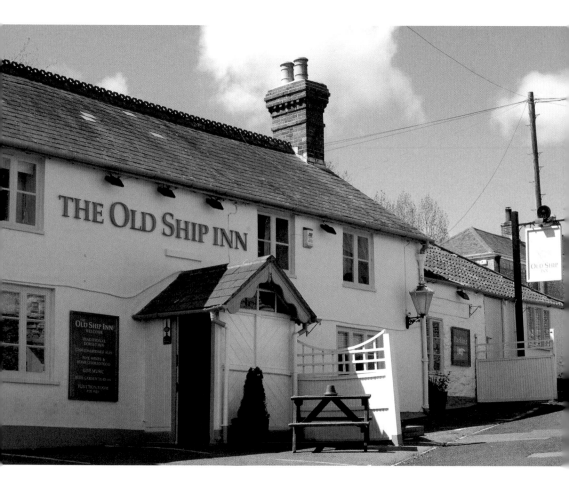

Upwey, the Old Ship Inn

Dick and Fancy leave Budmouth for Mellstock. Hardy says that there is 'a good inn, "The Ship", four miles out of Budmouth', where Dick broke his journeys between Mellstock and Budmouth on the outward and return legs, and here they stop. This must be what Hardy had in mind, the real Old Ship Inn at Upwey, not only the right distance from Weymouth but also at the bottom of the crossing of the South Dorset Ridgeway that separates Weymouth from the Dorset hinterland, making it a good place to rest or prepare for a climb!

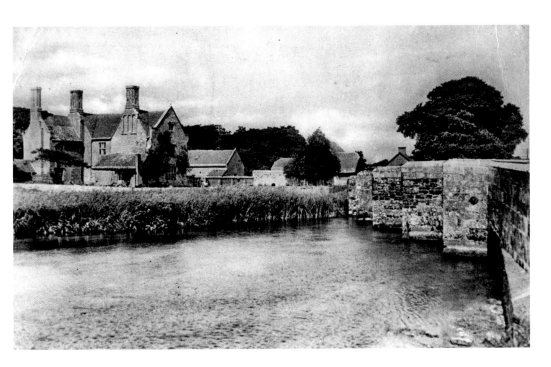

Wool, Woolbridge Manor and Bridge over the Frome

In *Tess of the D'Urbervilles*, Tess and Angel Clare spend their unhappy honeymoon at Wellbridge Manor, getting there from the nearby village by crossing the 'great Elizabethan bridge'. This is indeed how to get to Woolbridge Manor from the village of Wool, which is some 10 miles east of Dorchester. Today they would have to proceed on foot, as the bridge is closed to traffic.

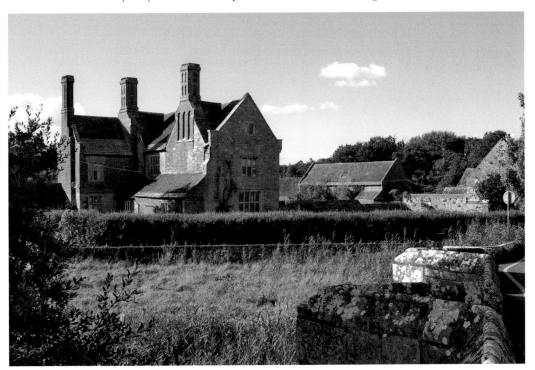

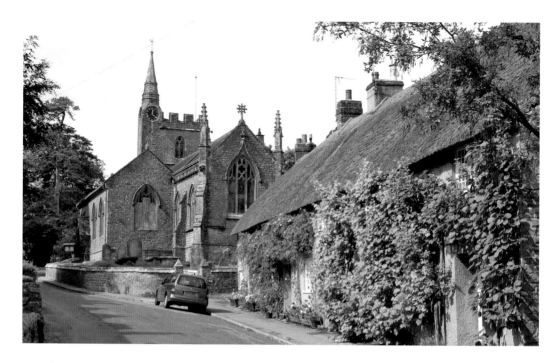

Evershot, Acorn Inn and the Village

Later, Tess goes in search of news of her husband, heading across country to Angel's father at Emminster. Her long walk takes her through 'Evershead', where in stopping for breakfast it is stated that she did not visit the Sow-and-Acorn because she 'avoided inns'. The picturesque Evershot not only matches the name, it also matches the location on Tess's route, and here the Acorn Inn proudly advertises its Hardy connection!

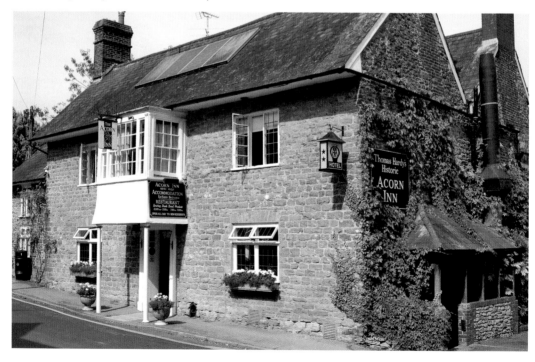

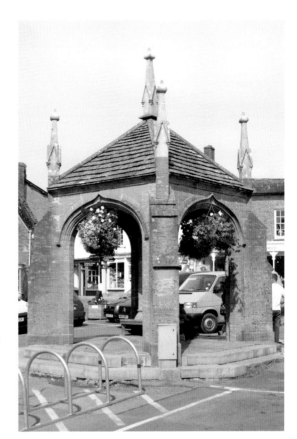

Beaminster, Views in and Around the Square

Emminster is described as lying in a basin, and indeed the little market town of Beaminster on which it is based has a spectacular location in a bowl among the west Dorset hills. Here are some views of the central square and its surrounds, through which any traveller would pass.

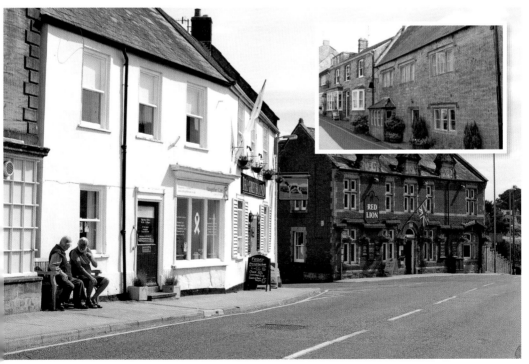

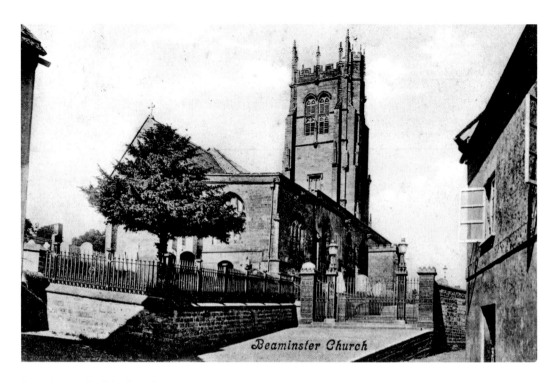

Beaminster, Parish Church, c. 1900
Tess's visit takes place on a Sunday, and she finds that the senior Clare, the local vicar, is conducting a service at the parish church. When she gets there, she finds the congregation leaving the church, and circumstances prevent her from meeting Angel's father. Here is Beaminster's parish church, located a short distance from the Square down Church Street. The older picture was taken about ten years after the novel was written, and perhaps a quarter-century after the time in which it was set.

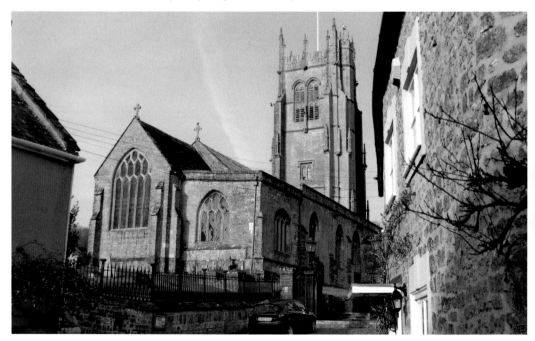

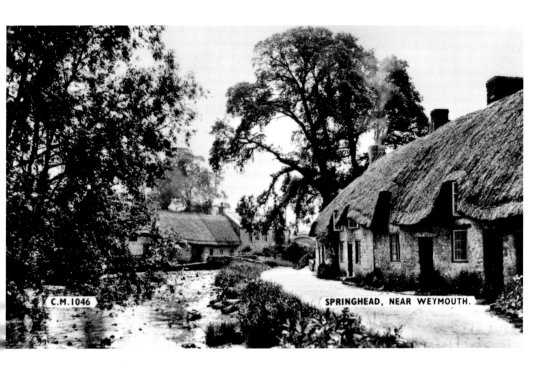

C.M.1046   SPRINGHEAD, NEAR WEYMOUTH.

Sutton Poyntz, Pond and Cottages, *c.* 1930

Much of the narrative in *The Trumpet Major* is set in 'Overcombe'. This is based on Sutton Poyntz, which lies beneath the South Dorset Ridgeway. Although today the suburbs of Weymouth have extended so far north-east that they reach the place, it still feels like a separate village. The eponymous hero John Loveday's father owned the mill at Overcombe, and here is Sutton Poyntz's millpond, together with cottages that have seen some changes.

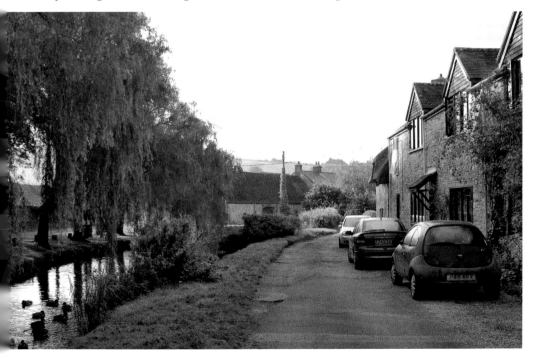

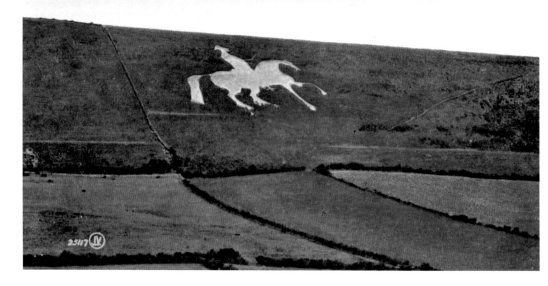

Osmington, White Horse, c. 1920
At one point John Loveday and his love see the cutting of a White Horse in a nearby chalk hillside. This is said to be a celebration of the naval victory at Trafalgar in 1805. The real Osmington White Horse lies not far east of Sutton Poyntz and, as recent research has shown, was actually cut in 1808 in celebration of its rider, King George III, and his patronage of Weymouth.

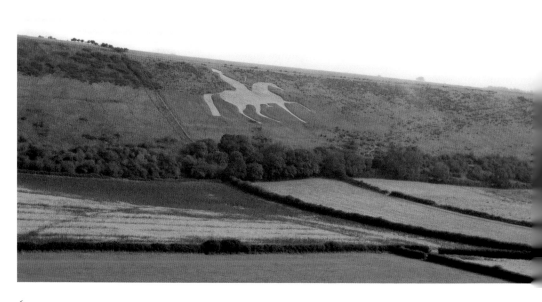

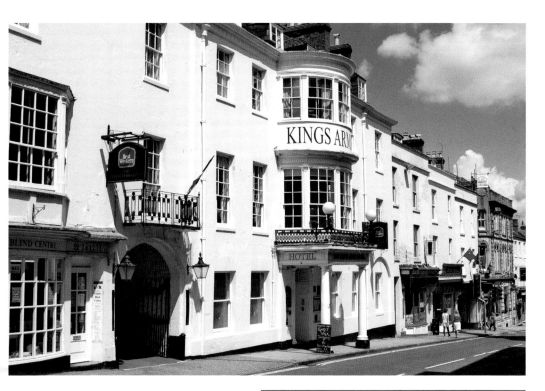

Dorchester, King's Arms

The Mayor of Casterbridge is largely set in that town, our Dorchester. Many of the buildings and features of the real town appear in the novel, often with their real names, and perhaps the best example is the King's Arms. The mayor, Michael Henchard, conducts much of his business here, and it is where his bankruptcy hearing is held. The King's Arms also appears in other works, including *Under the Greenwood Tree* and *Tess of the D'Urbervilles*.

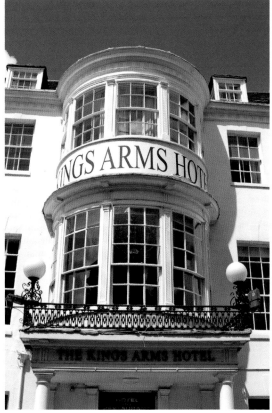

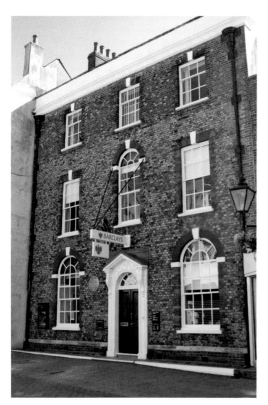

Dorchester, Barclays Bank and Corn Exchange

Here are two more examples. Barclays Bank (*above*) in South Street dates from around 1780 and is generally recognised as being the model for Henchard's home. The Corn Exchange (*below*) is given its real name in the novel. It is the work of Benjamin Ferrey, who has already been mentioned, and was built in 1847–48, making it perhaps less than a decade old when the novel's main action takes place. The little clock tower was not added until 1864.

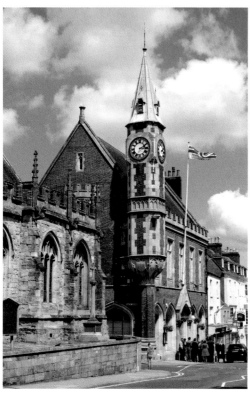

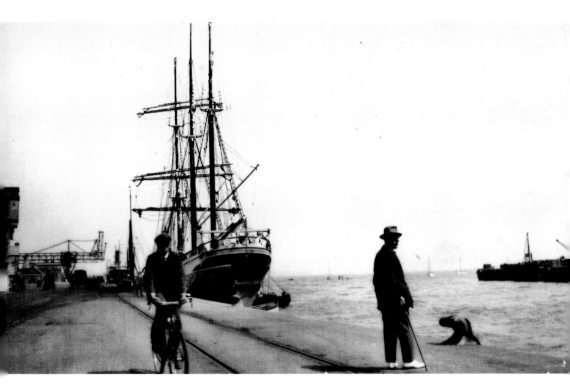

Poole, the Quay, *c.* 1930
In the latter stages of *The Mayor of Casterbridge*, the sailor Richard Newson returns to the country through 'Havenpool'. This old picture was probably taken just after Hardy's death, but it still shows a busy trading port, just as it was nearly a century before when Newson would have landed. Today much more of the activity is about leisure.

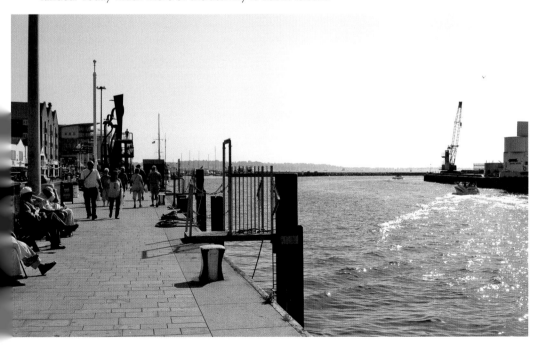

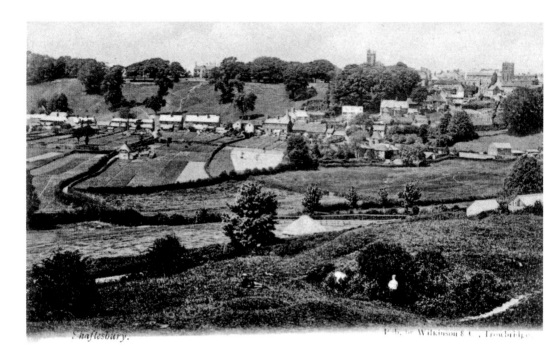

Shaftesbury, View of the Town, c. 1905

At the beginning of Part 4 of *Jude the Obscure*, Jude goes in search of Sue Phillotson at Shaston. Here Hardy gives a very accurate description of the real hilltop town of Shaftesbury, in north Dorset close to the Wiltshire border. Even 'Shaston' is an old alternative name for Shaftesbury, and he also calls it 'Palladour', a mythical name for a prehistoric town here. These pictures look towards the town from the south, with the suburb of St James strung out along the base of the hill.

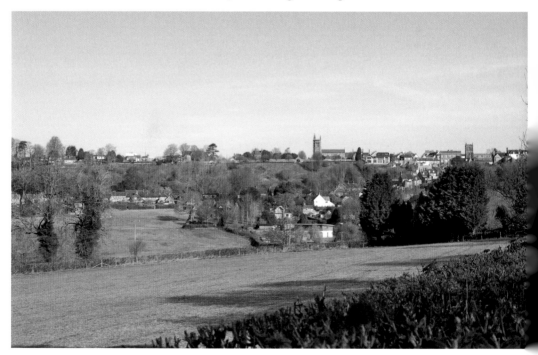

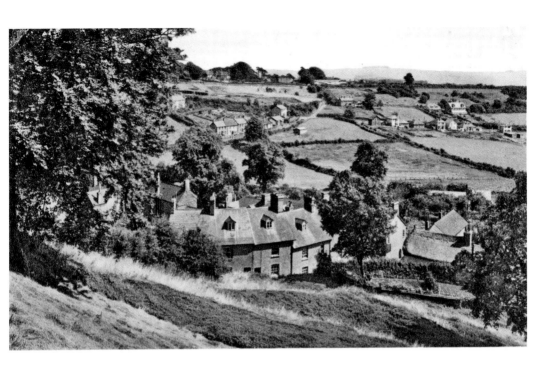

Shaftesbury, View from Park Walk, *c.* 1935

Sue lives in Abbey Walk, the real name of a street on the west side of the site of the medieval Abbey, which as Hardy says had been completely levelled by his day. These views look from Park Walk on the south side of the Abbey site, with houses in the famous Gold Hill in the foreground of the old shot. These houses are obscured by vegetation in my photograph, which also shows how the town has expanded across the high ground to the east.

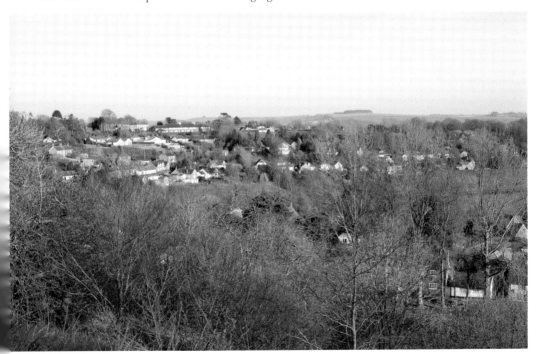

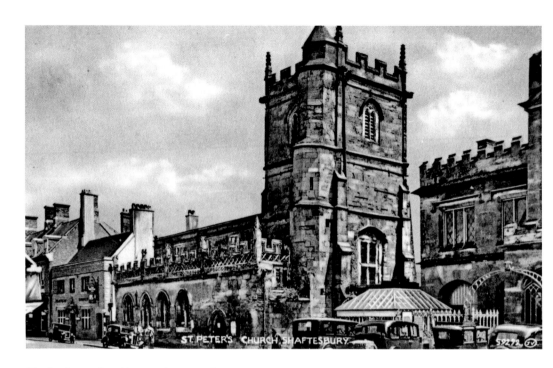

Shaftesbury, the Mitre and St Peter's, c. 1930
In this novel Hardy tells a good local story. He says that after the Reformation the townspeople were so destitute that they could not pay for priests and so had to pull their churches down. They then spent their leisure time (and money) in the local pubs bemoaning this situation! The Mitre Inn, on the left here, is one such establishment, although the surviving late medieval church of St Peter next door is clear proof that this is just a tale, as Hardy well knew.

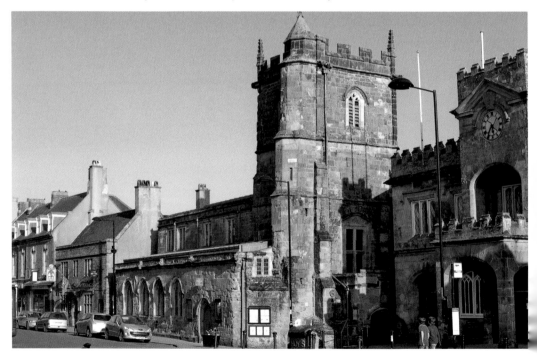

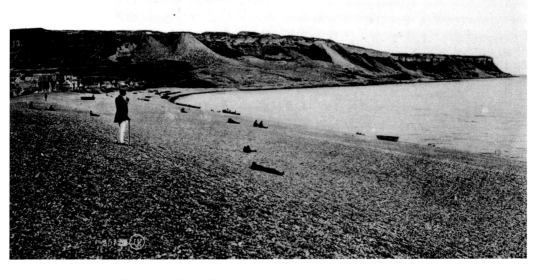

Portland, View from Chesil Beach, c. 1905

The island of Portland is the real star of one of Hardy's less well-known novels, *The Well-Beloved*. He calls it 'The Isle of Slingers' in recognition of the islanders' ancient skill in defending themselves with sling-stones. This view looks from Chesil Beach towards the main mass of the island, particularly the cliffs at West Weares. Between the times of the two photographs, the beach has been raised for sea defence purposes, and at left, the expansion of the village of Chesil has displaced the stone-walled fields.

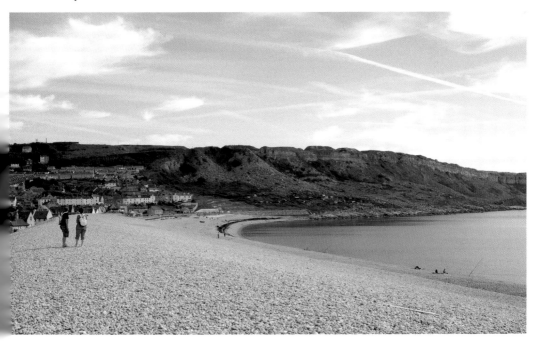

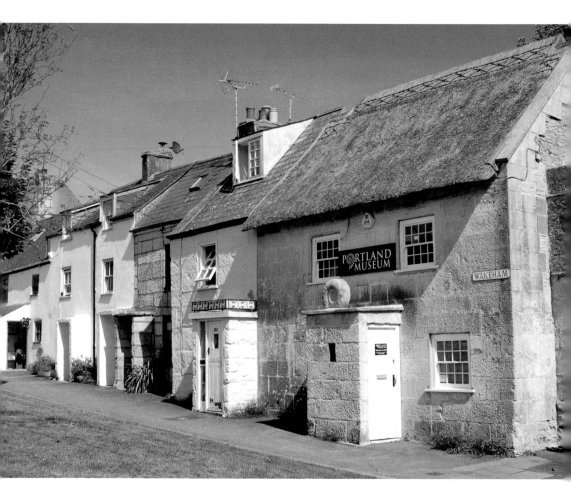

Portland, Museum at Wakeham

The Well-Beloved tells the story of a sculptor, Jonathan Pierston, who over the course of his life falls in love with three women named Avice Caro – they being mother, daughter, and granddaughter. The cottage home of the first Avice is described early in the novel and is said to be based on the one that now houses Portland Museum. The museum was founded in 1929 by Marie Stopes, best known otherwise as a birth control pioneer, who was a friend of Hardy's.

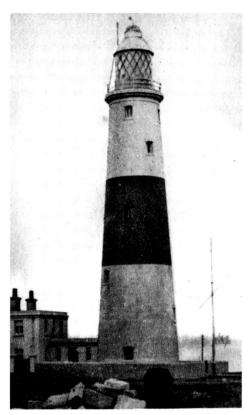

Portland, Lighthouse at the Bill, *c.* 1920
The southern tip of the island is Portland Bill,
although Hardy says that its real name is the
Beal and only 'strangers' (presumably meaning
non-Portlanders) call it 'the Bill'. Here we see
the lighthouse and coastguard accommodation
that were officially opened in 1906, and
which replaced the Old Higher and Lower
Lighthouses that had been built further back
from the headland in 1869.

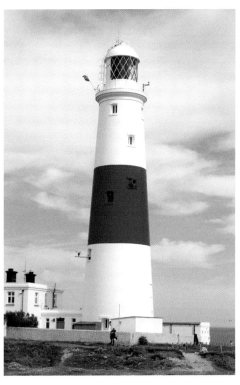

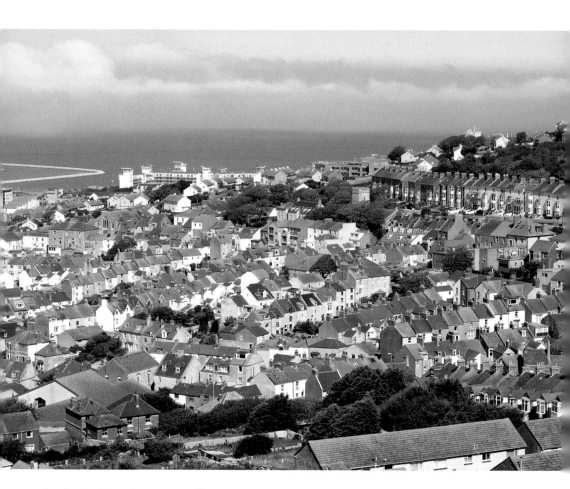

Portland, View of Fortuneswell

One afternoon Pierston and the eldest Avice visit Portland Bill, and their time together is cut short because Avice has to give a recitation in the Street of Wells. Hardy describes this place as 'the village commanding the entrance to the island', which has since become a town. Here is the real Fortuneswell, which fits Hardy's description admirably. A great deal of the housing we see here was built in Hardy's lifetime.

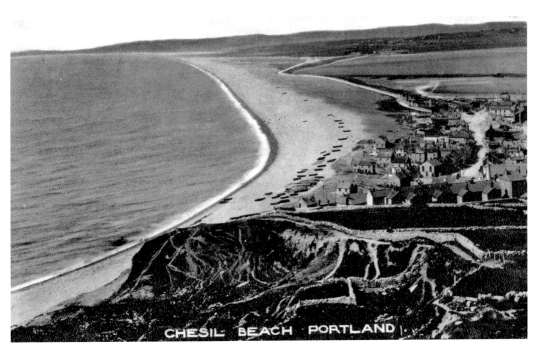

CHESIL BEACH PORTLAND

Portland, View Down to Chesil Beach, *c.* 1905

This view looks down across Chesil Beach (or 'Pebble Beach' to Hardy) from the top of the island. In a scene that marks the beginning of the end of his relationship with the first Avice, Pierston walks along the road beside Chesil Beach towards Budmouth one evening. He meets a Miss Bencomb, and when the weather worsens they take shelter under a lerret, one of the distinctive double-ended fishing boats of Chesil Beach. A number of these can be seen drawn up beside Chesil village in the old picture.

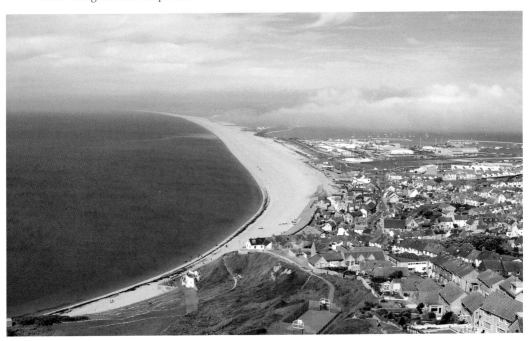

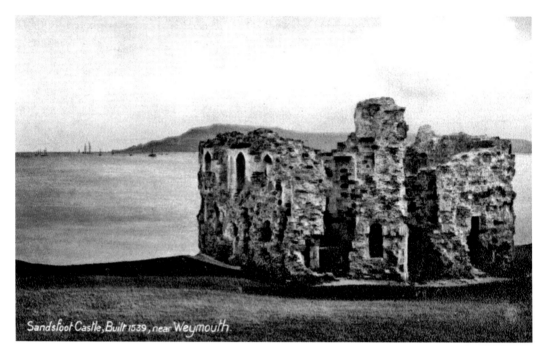

Sandsfoot Castle, Built 1539, near Weymouth

Weymouth, Sandsfoot Castle, *c.* 1910

Pierston's original plan had been to undertake this walk with Avice, who would accompany him as far as 'Henry the Eighth's Castle above the sands'. Hardy must have in mind Sandsfoot Castle on the Weymouth side of Portland Harbour, which was constructed around 1541 as part of that monarch's fortification of the South Coast. Like the Osmington White Horse, it has been restored recently.

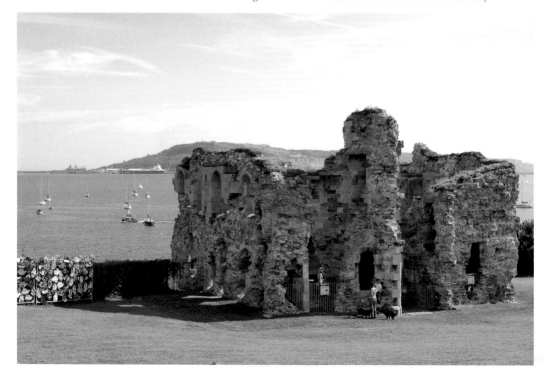

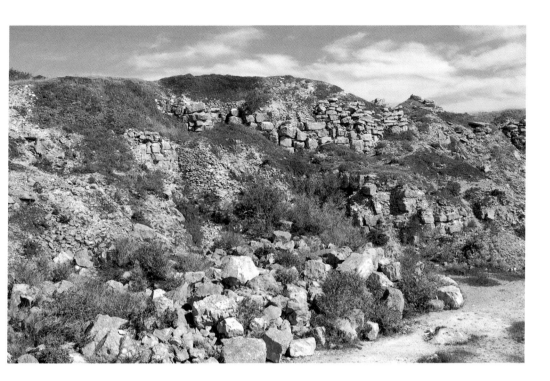

Portland, Quarried Landscape

Jonathan Pierston's father had made the family's fortune through quarrying. The large-scale quarrying of the limestone of Portland had begun in the seventeenth century, much of it being used in London, and by Hardy's day a great deal of the upper part of the island was being worked. In contrast to the techniques used today, the methods used in the nineteenth century left a distinctive landscape of cuttings, trackways and banks of quarry waste called 'beaches'.

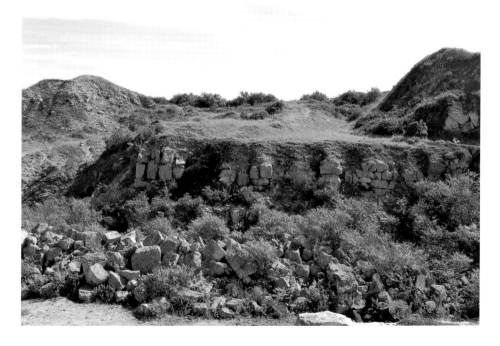

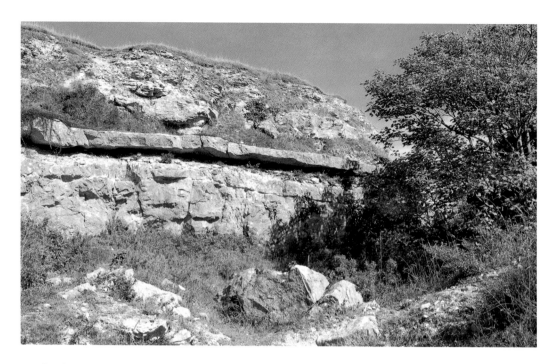

Portland, Quarried Landscape

The Pierstons had quarried in the east of the island, but today the best survivals of the nineteenth-century stone quarrying landscape are generally further north on Portland, in quarries such as Tout, Weycroft and Kingbarrow. They can seem like a cross between a Mediterranean scene and a moonscape. The quarrymen sometimes deliberately showed off their skills – the tunnel that linked Weycroft and Kingbarrow quarries (*below*) is a fine example of their workmanship.

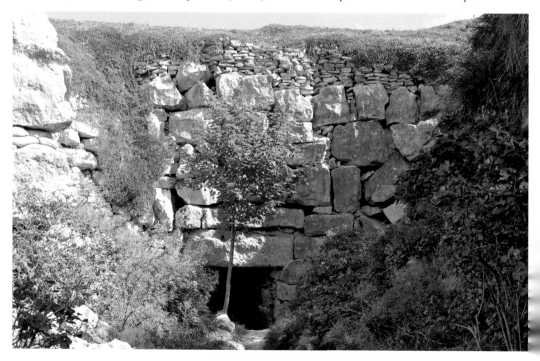

Other Towns and Villages That Appear in Hardy's Writing

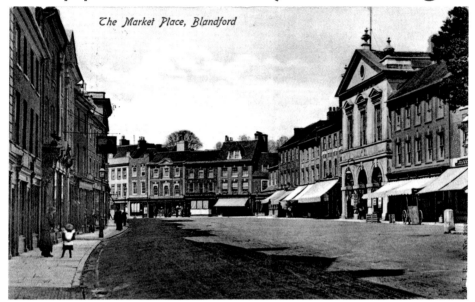

The Market Place, Blandford

Blandford Forum, Market Place, c. 1900

Blandford Forum lies some 17 miles north-east of Dorchester, and appears in Hardy as Shottsford Forum. Here we see one of the best sights in the town, the broad Market Place surrounded by Georgian buildings, including the town hall on the right. There was a major fire in the town in 1731, and fortunately for us, but not the inhabitants at the time, almost the whole town had to be rebuilt. The architects of much of this work were the brothers William and John Bastard.

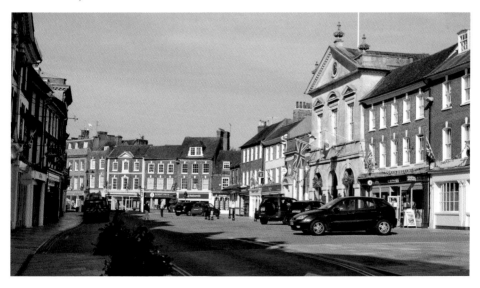

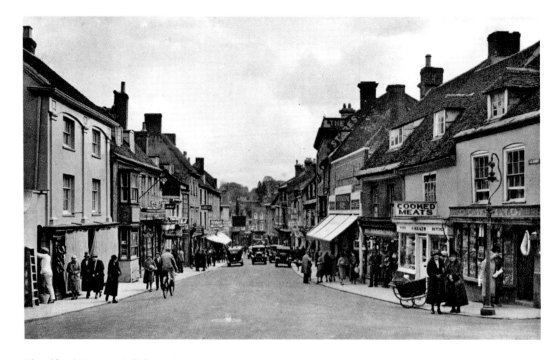

Blandford Forum, Salisbury Street, c. 1935
The junction of Salisbury Street and the Market Place is the corner just right of centre in the previous view. Now we go up Salisbury Street and look back down to the Market Place to see a good selection of the more functional and domestic Georgian buildings of the town. There seems to have been only one significant change over the past three quarters of a century.

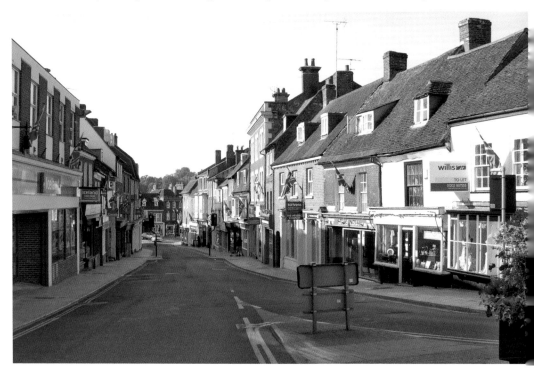

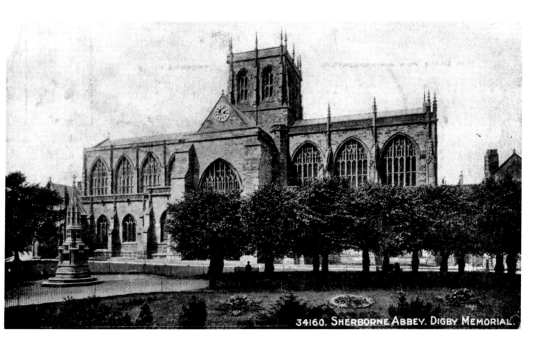

34160. SHERBORNE ABBEY. DIGBY MEMORIAL.

Sherborne, the Abbey, *c.* 1910

Again about 17 miles from Dorchester, but this time northwards and close to the Somerset border, we find Sherborne. Hardy calls it 'Sherton Abbas' in recognition of its superb Abbey church, which we see here. The Digby Memorial is on the left in these views. It was erected in 1884 to George Digby Wingfield Digby of Sherborne Castle, who funded major restoration work on the Abbey, most of which took place in the 1850s.

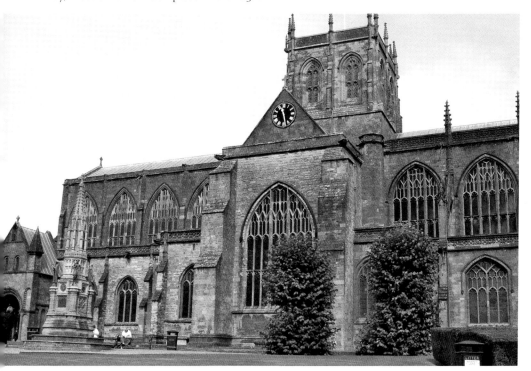

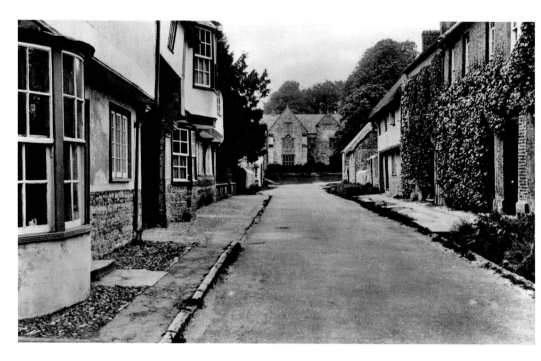

Cerne Abbas, Abbey Street, c. 1930

Here is a real 'Abbas', which lies about 7 miles north of Dorchester. Hardy calls it 'Abbot's Cernel', almost a reversal of the real name and recognition of the importance of Cerne Abbey in the place's history. At the far end of this view we see Abbey House, which incorporates part of the Abbey's fifteenth-century gatehouse.

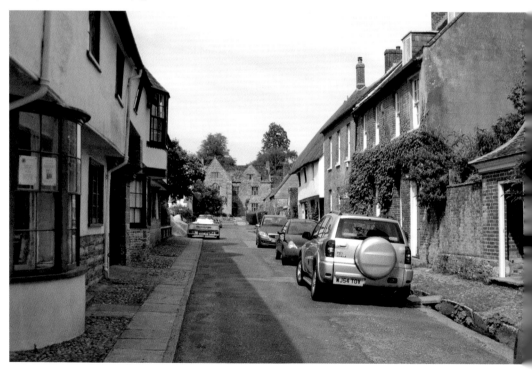

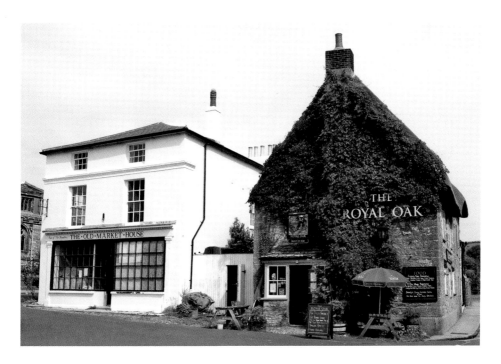

Cerne Abbas, Village Views and the Giant

Now for some other images of Cerne Abbas. There are lots of old stone buildings here and the material for them was easily obtained; after Henry VIII's Dissolution of the Monasteries local builders used the Abbey complex as a quarry. The Cerne Abbas Giant sits on the hillside above the village and is a major tourist attraction. Of the various explanations of its origin, I prefer the one that it was the local landowner's send-up of Oliver Cromwell.

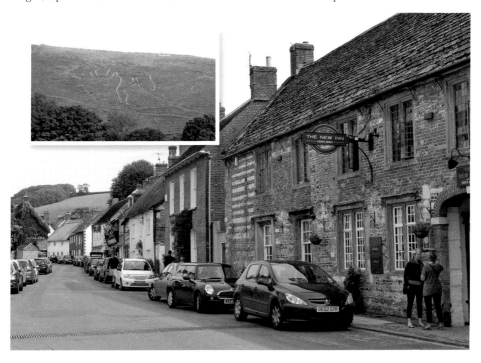

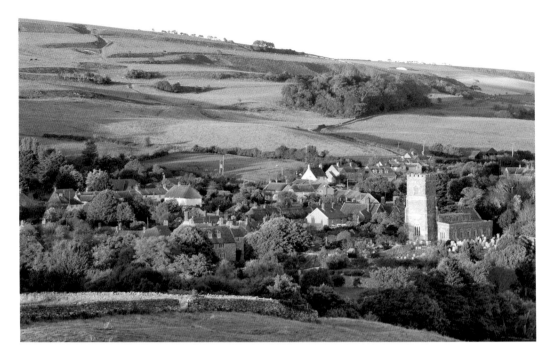

Abbotsbury, Village and Abbey Ruins

Abbotsbury is a similar distance from Dorchester to Cerne Abbas, this time in a south-westerly direction. It lies near the north-western end of Pebble or Chesil Beach, and like Cerne Abbas its name reflects the historic importance of its Abbey. Hardy recognised the village's Abbey and location by using the names 'Abbotsea' and 'Abbot's Beach'. Here we see views of the village and part of the Abbey ruins.

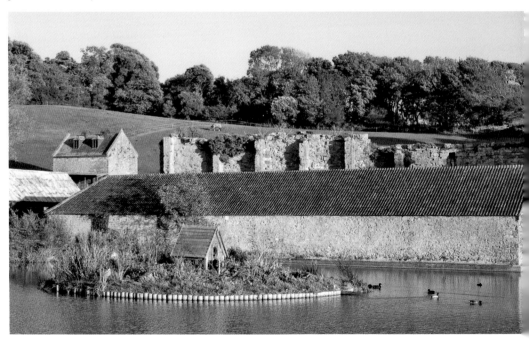

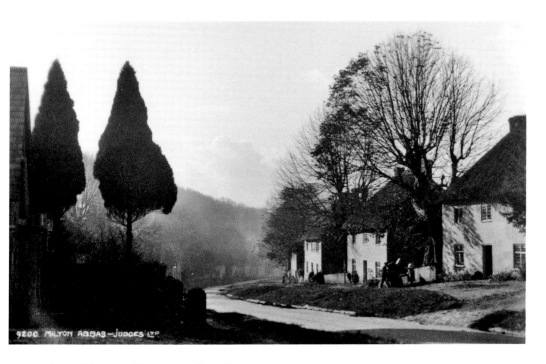

Milton Abbas, Looking Down the Village, *c.* 1925

Hardy's name for Milton Abbas is the doubly accurate 'Middleton'. Firstly because the village occupies a central location in Dorset, and secondly since that was a real name of the town here that was demolished in the late eighteenth century to make way for a lake and landscaped garden for the local mansion. These pictures look down the village street from near the Hambro Arms pub.

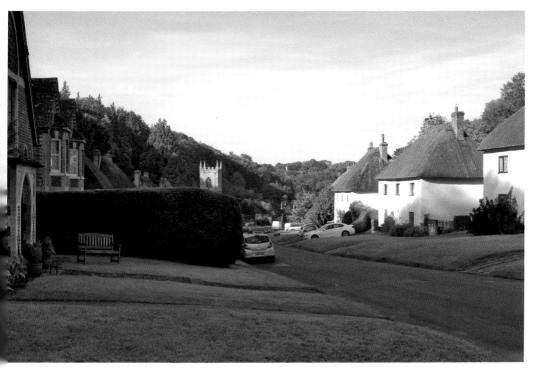

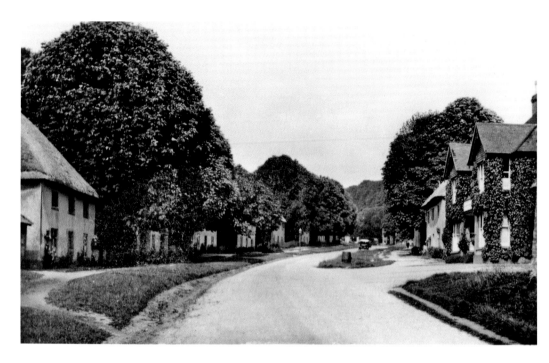

Milton Abbas, Looking Upwards, *c.* 1930
Here is a view looking back from further down the village street. Most of the cottages the inhabitants of the old town were moved into were identical and very picturesque, but their new gardens on the steep slopes behind their homes were not good for growing the produce that was an important part of their diets.

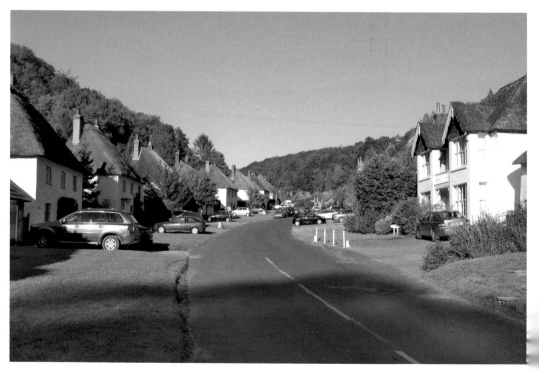

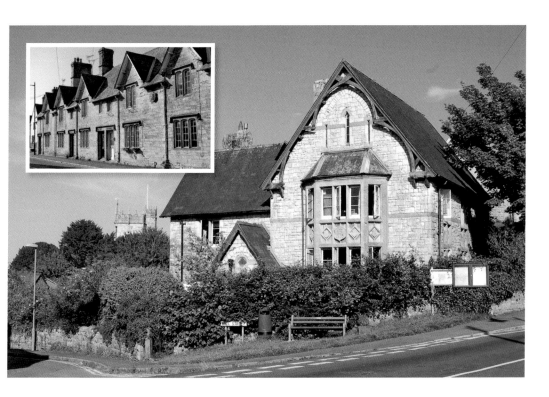

Puddletown

Puddletown lies only a couple of miles north-east of Hardy's birthplace, and relatives on his mother's side lived here. It appears in his novels as 'Weatherbury', which is a slight variation of 'Weatherby', the real name of an Iron Age hillfort a few miles further away. Many of the buildings, especially along the main road, were built in the 1860s and 1870s by the local squire.

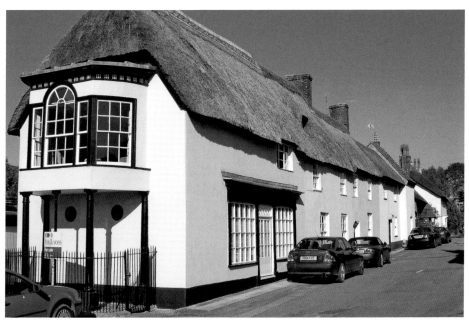

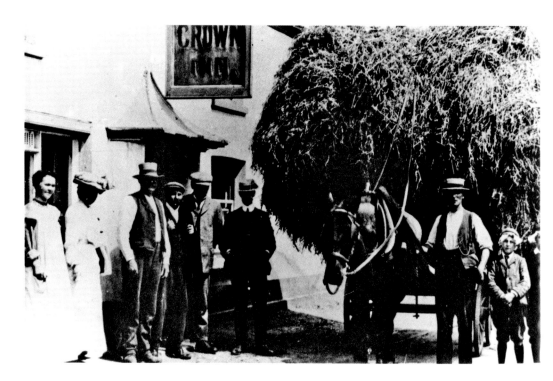

Tolpuddle, the Crown Inn, *c.* 1900

Tolpuddle is the next sizeable village down the Piddle from Puddletown. Although it is more renowned for the Tolpuddle Martyrs, it appears in *Desperate Remedies* as 'Tolchurch', and this scene outside the village pub seems reminiscent of a Hardy novel. The Crown burned down in the mid-twentieth century, and its replacement, the Martyrs Inn, was formally opened by the TUC General Secretary in 1971.

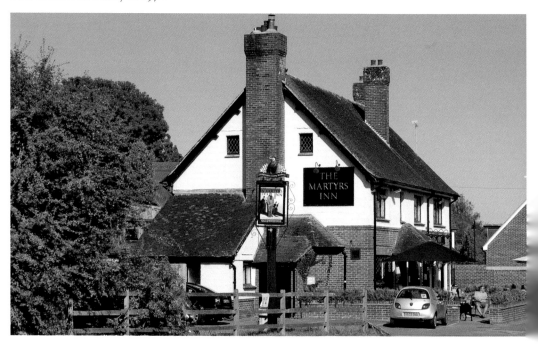

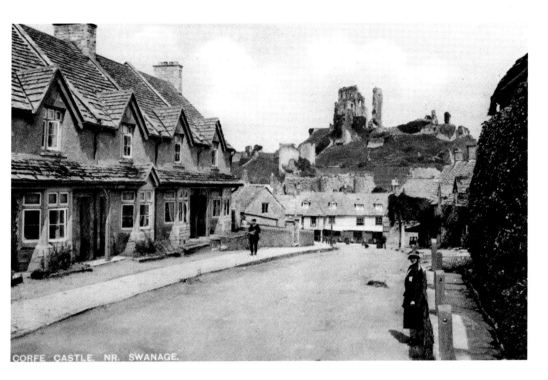

CORFE CASTLE, NR. SWANAGE.

Corfe Castle, View of the Castle from East Street, c. 1925
Hardy chose the name 'Corvsgate' for Corfe Castle, and it is a good one. The great medieval castle guards a gap in the Purbeck Hills that is indeed a gateway into the Isle of Purbeck. Here we see one of the classic views of the castle and village of the same name, looking from the main road towards the Greyhound pub in the Square.

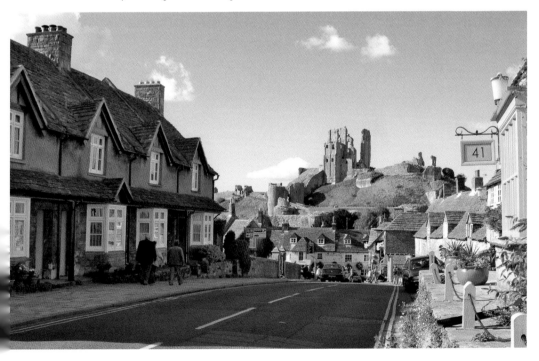

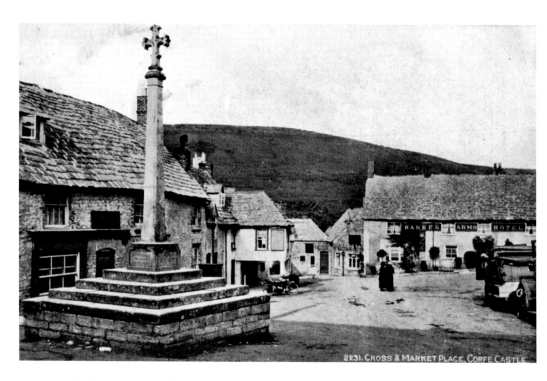

Corfe Castle, the Cross and the Square, _c._ 1925

Next we go round the corner into the Square. The cross here was erected in 1897 in celebration of Queen Victoria's Diamond Jubilee, probably on an earlier base. Beyond it we can see the projecting porch on the Greyhound and on the right is the Bankes Arms.

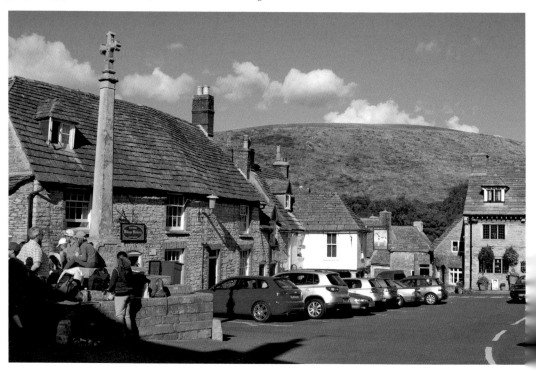

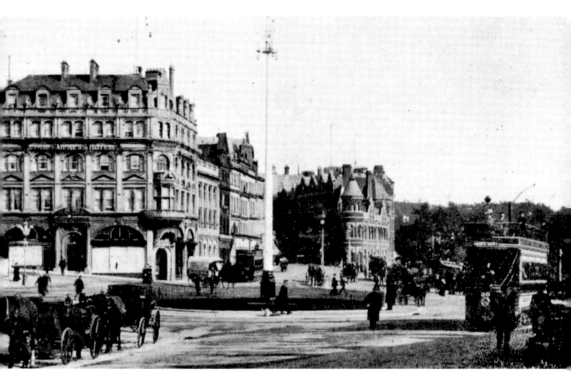

Bournemouth, the Square, c. 1905

Bournemouth was not in Dorset during Hardy's lifetime. I have included it in this book not only because it now is (it was transferred from Hampshire in 1974), but because as 'Sandbourne' it appears in several novels. Here we see some of the late Victorian development in the town centre that testified to the prosperity of this resort during Hardy's lifetime.

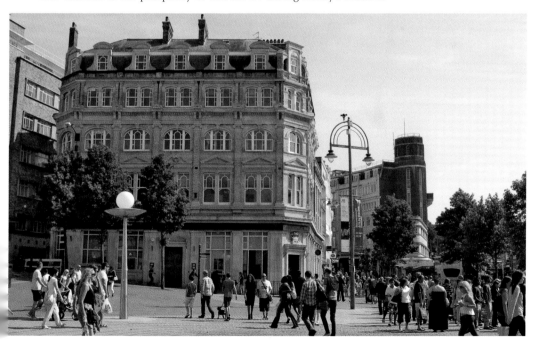

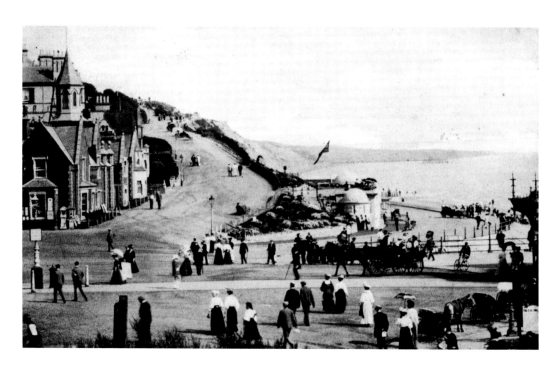

Bournemouth, Entrance to Pier and East Cliff, c. 1910

In *Tess of the D'Urbervilles*, Angel Clare comes to Sandbourne in search of Tess. Angel is surprised by the huge contrast between Sandbourne, which has all the latest accoutrements of a 'fashionable watering-place', and 'Egdon Waste', the heathlands that once stretched this far from the Dorchester area, and which he has just crossed. Many contemporaries who saw Bournemouth expanding rapidly, literally from nothing, during the course of the nineteenth century must have shared his feelings.

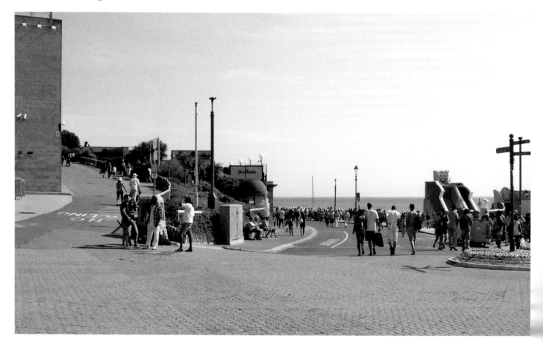

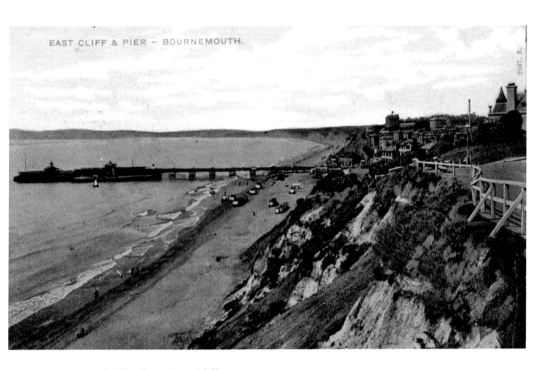

Bournemouth, Pier from East Cliff, *c.* 1900

Here we look westwards to see Bournemouth Pier jutting out into the broad sweep of Poole Bay. The pier appears in *The Hand of Ethelberta*, much of which is set in the town. In fact, there were several piers during Hardy's lifetime. A jetty constructed in 1856 was soon found to be too small, and a bigger pier replaced it five years later. This in turn had to be rebuilt nearly twenty years later, and extensions were then added on two occasions.

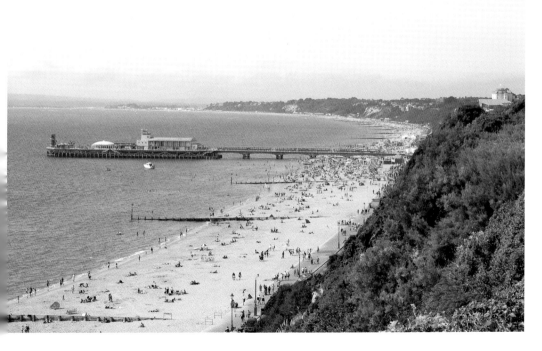

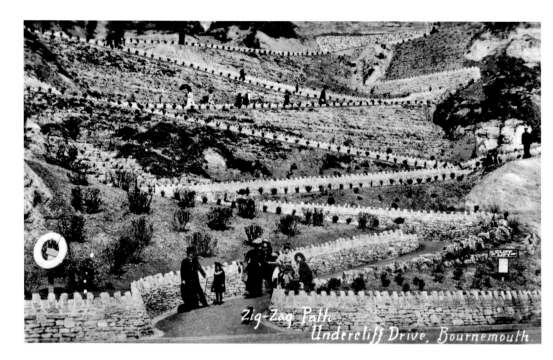

Bournemouth, Zigzag Path, *c.* 1910

There are several zigzag paths that link the cliff top with the beach along the seafront from Branksome to Boscombe. This one goes down East Cliff, close to the location from which the previous views were taken. The size of the ornamental planting in the old photograph suggests the path had been constructed quite recently.

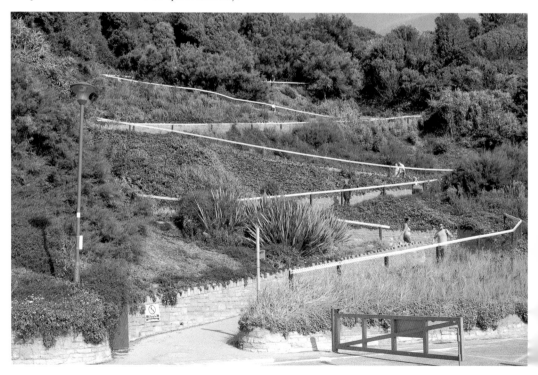

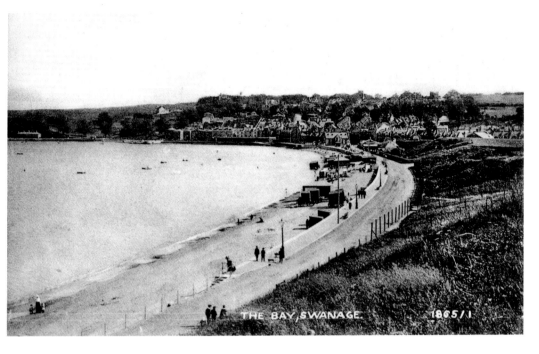

Swanage, Looking South Around the Bay, *c.* 1910

Much of the later part of *The Hand of Ethelberta* takes place in Swanage, around Poole Bay from Bournemouth near the south-east corner of the Isle of Purbeck. Hardy and his first wife, Emma, lived here for about a year from 1875 while he was researching for the novel, lodging with a retired sea captain. He gives it the name 'Knollsea'.

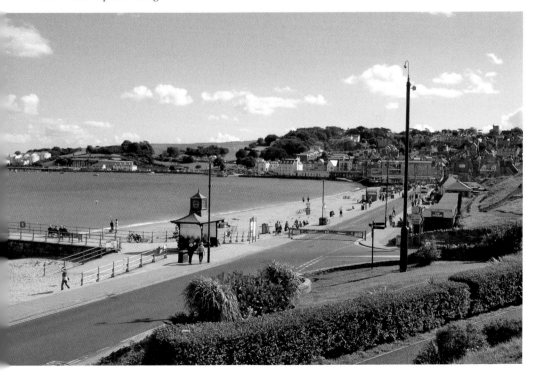

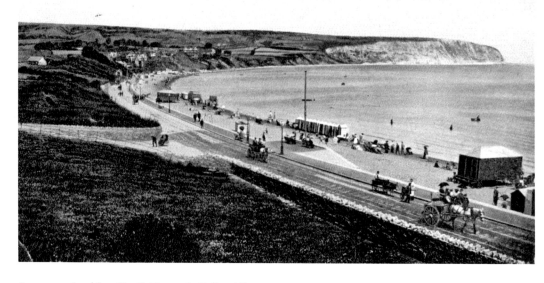

Swanage, Looking North Towards Ballard Down, *c.* 1910

Hardy says of 'Knollsea' that the inhabitants made their living either from fishing or quarrying
– much of the stone quarried in Purbeck was shipped out from Swanage, often to London. When
he was there in the 1870s the local tourism industry was in its infancy, but as the old picture
shows it was flourishing in Edwardian times. There are bathing machines and lots of other
activity on the beach, and seaside villas are spreading around the north side of the bay.

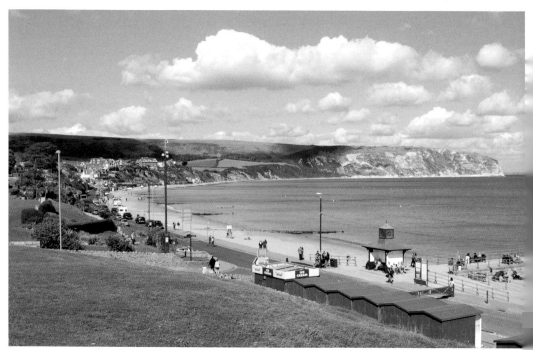

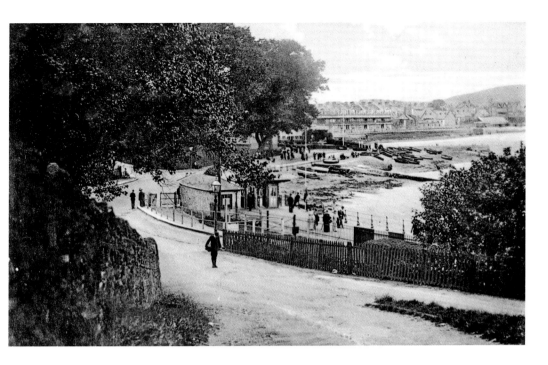

Swanage, Pier Entrance, *c.* 1920

We now move round past the town centre to a path that runs uphill beside Prince Albert Gardens. We are looking back at the booths at the entrance to Swanage Pier. A pier was built here in 1859/60 solely for the transfer of quarried stone into ships. Things began to change in 1874 (the year before Hardy came here) when a steamer service from Bournemouth and Poole began using the pier, which encouraged daytrips from those resorts. In the 1890s the number of visitors was so great that a bigger pier had to be built.

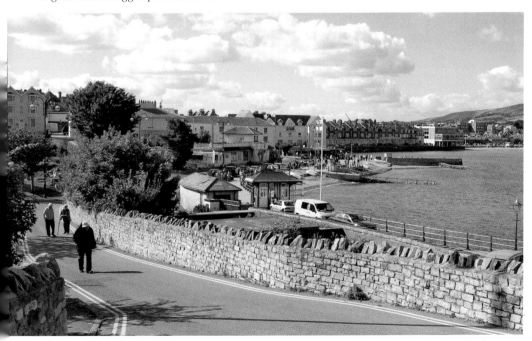

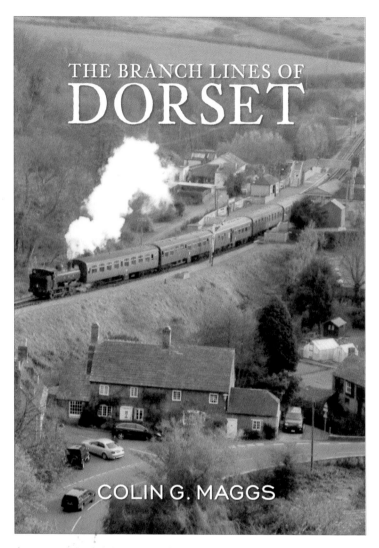

The Branch Lines of Dorset

Colin Maggs

All the Dorset Branches are described in this absorbing, entertaining
and well-researched book.

978 1 84868 352 5
160 pages

Available from all good bookshops or order direct
from our website www.amberleybooks.com